We the People
Are the Messiah

Deborah and Jack Bartello

Project Enlightenment Press
Mount Shasta, California, USA

We the People Are the Messiah
by
Deborah and Jack Bartello

Published in 1999

Copyright © 1998   Deborah and Jack Bartello

All stories in this book are true. However, to protect the privacy of our clients and students, the names used are not their real names.

00 99 98   0 9 8 7 6 5 4 3 2 1

Published by
PROJECT ENLIGHTENMENT PRESS
PO BOX 1497
MT. SHASTA, CA 96067
Toll-free: (800) 446-5959 (Orders only)
PHONE: (530) 926-1714
FAX: (530) 926-1769
INTERNET: www.projectenlightenment.com
EMAIL: jd@projectenlightenment.com

Cover photograph by Pan Brian Paine

Cover design by Quicksilver Productions

ISBN 0-9668252-1-7

Printed in the USA

CONTENTS

ACKNOWLEDGMENTS

We offer our most heartfelt thanks to those, seen and unseen, who have contributed to the creation of this material. You know who you are. We are most grateful to you.

A NOTE FROM THE AUTHORS

This is a book about Jesus, his life two thousand years ago and the roles he has played in our lives, both then and now. This book is equally about you, the reader—your love for yourself and your Creator. It is about your relationship to, and ownership of, your truly beautiful, powerful and wise God-Self. It is about your own personal freedom and sacredness.

In the following pages you will read about our experiences with Jesus personally, professionally and with our extended family of workshop participants. We are not born-again Christians and are not affiliated with any religious organization. We are simply two people who had extraordinary experiences with Jesus that were unsolicited, and yet profound. We found in sharing them with others that they were greatly affected as well.

Fifteen years ago we began doing healing and facilitation work with other people on a professional basis. We had both traveled far on our own spiritual journeys and the next step after coming together as a couple was to join our love for spirit and put it forth in our spiritual teaching and private work, assisting others on their journeys. This we knew would deepen our own connection with ourselves and each other as well as enable us to live what we truly believed and felt was meaningful.

We started out by teaching people about energy, pure and simple. We taught them how to feel energy, read energy and move energy. It was obvious that without this base of sensitivity well established and activated within, there was no way people were going to be able to interpret and understand their emerging spiritual experiences. Learning about energy was the way to begin the discourse between self and spirit, and strengthening these skills would be an ongoing requirement as each person matured in his or her own self-awareness. Through this language of energy we knew from our own experience that the spiritual worlds would open quickly and effortlessly.

The second phase of our work focused on clearing and healing. Just as the language of energy was essential to one's spiritual movement, it was also obvious that cleansing and clearing the way inside for these higher frequencies was also essential. Without attention paid to this part of the equation, the incoming spiritual energies would have no room within which to engage, integrate and flow. It would be like trying to pour fresh, clear, clean water into a cup already full with old, stagnant water. We recognized the benefits of "flushing out" the spiritual and emotional pipes.

After many years of doing clearing work, both on ourselves and others, we were spent. We knew this work had been extremely important and beneficial, but we also knew there was more for us to discover. "What," we asked ourselves, "was the purpose of all this preparation?" Asking this question prompted a leap into a level of refined energy with which we had not previously been connected. We found ourselves letting go of our business of healing people so that we could make room for this new energy to enter more fully.

Our emphasis shifted from healing and clearing to empowering others to heal and transform themselves. Our message to them was that they needed to take full responsibility for their own healing journey. It seemed as though we were blasting open a world within us that had been quietly contained. Our work became much deeper, more challenging and more exciting. Ironically, with this shift into these new depths, our audiences became smaller. With this decrease in numbers, we flourished with even greater depth and intimacy. We knew we were taking risks by leaping into the unknown and by following this more refined and demanding path of spirit but there was no other choice we would have ever considered.

It was at this time in our development that Jesus came sweeping into our lives. As you will read throughout the pages of this book, his entry into our field changed us forever. There was no denying the intensity of his purpose with us and there was no hesitation on our part about embracing him and whatever he wanted. It was brand new territory for us, and yet we came to find out it was "as old as the hills."

We offer you this book because we have seen in ourselves and others that there is now a place and need for it. Whenever someone asks us what this book is about, we tell them it is about Jesus. The reactions that we get are usually one of two: a hushed and reverent, "tell me more," or a frigid cold-shoulder, a turning away as if we had never spoken. The subject of Jesus has very little gray area for most of us who have been raised in a Christian ethic. As you will read, it is a loaded subject and one about which much more will be written in the future. The "Jesus box" has been opened and it is here for all of us to look into. What concepts, baggage, projections, feelings, assumptions do you have lingering in the attics of your mind about him? Shall you look or not look? What is to be gained by "covering old ground?" This book offers you some answers to these questions.

Many of us are hungry for this material. We are hungry to re-evaluate ourselves and base our lives on what is meaningful. We are hungry to revise our belief systems to reflect what we have always known inside—that we are all God-Beings, Free-Beings and love-centered Beings. Jesus is a catalyst through which we can all see and know ourselves more deeply.

Our book is a simply a message of love. What propelled us to write it was the belief that we, as a western civilization, need to "come clean" with this subject matter. Our intention is to bring it all back home to Self so that we can have and embrace our own unique experience of Jesus without any of the external man-made limitations and dogma attached to him. In doing so, we can once again open our hearts to the depth of love that he so richly represents.

To those who want to realize their true dreams, to those who "walk their talk," to the courageous and fiery individuals who wish to live more fully—this book is for you. Some of you may already feel fulfilled and complete—more power to you! This book will simply add extra fire to that gusto and glory you already know.

Throughout this book, we make reference to God and to each of us as God. We are not speaking here of God as the judge, the scorekeeper and the task master, but rather as our divine energy, our life force, the spirit that moves in all things, the pulse of

Creation. We are sourced by God, therefore we are God also. Knowing ourselves as God is not our egos talking. It is the truth of our Being—plain and simple. Jesus showed us this so beautifully.

This book is about breaking old ground and birthing new. It speaks to the pioneering spirit in each of us that has heard the call to forge new paths of freedom for ourselves and others. It concerns itself with joyously paving a new way of love for generations to come. We invite you to bring an open mind and an open heart to this material. If you do, we feel it will nourish and support you in ways that will truly astound you. This is our hope and our prayer for you. Enjoy!

Blessings Be.

I come to be with you now, Beloved.

Our love of long ago was never over,
Never torn, nor forsaken.

I come to you now because you know who I am.
I am your Brother.
I am your Friend.
I am your Soul.

Will you take a quiet walk with me now?

Will you share this journey of remembrance with me?

Let us be together, once again, in love.
In love where nothing else exists.

Quiet oneness. Gentle family.
Holy union.

Joy of heart.
Freedom of spirit.

Ours.
Yours and mine.
I come to you because you know who I am.
I Am You.

AN INVITATION FROM JESUS

"The purpose of this writing is to free up the many misconceptions which people have held about me through the ages. It is time now to demystify and clarify the entire human drama of the crucifixion and everything that I stood for at that time. I use the words "human drama" very deliberately since that is exactly what it has become.

"It has become a play through which individuals have sought to gain power for themselves and keep the masses in a blind state. It has been a play through which many have inadvertently diminished themselves. They have taken on guilt and repression in my name.

"Let it be understood now, the entire sequence of events was *my own responsibility*. I was the star on stage and everyone involved was in agreement with the play. I was not the victim. Let me say this one more time. *I WAS NOT THE VICTIM.*

"How many of you have held me in this position? How many of you have been angry and resentful and unforgiving of those who "did it" to me? How many of you have blamed yourselves for not doing something to stop it? How many of you have hardened your hearts so you wouldn't feel the pain? How many of you have blamed and resented me for leaving you?

"How many of you have shut off your own light and freedom because you felt and still feel that you will undergo the same punishment? How many of you would welcome the opportunity to return to that play of events so that you could understand them correctly this time and therefore unlock your own stored fear and misgivings?

"How many of you are ready to come out into the sunshine with me so that we can do it right this time? How many of you are ready to declare to yourselves the truth of your Christ within you? How many of you are willing to live this openly, proudly and joyously?

"If you have any response inside of you to any or all of these questions, then join me in the following pages so that we may get on with this revelation. Your time has come and so has mine.

"Hallelujah!"

Chapter One

Restoration to Love

It all started when Jesus came to us at the cabin in Mount Shasta. It was May, 1991, and we had decided to go into spiritual retreat for one month. As you may know, Mount Shasta is an "illuminated mountain," considered by many spiritual seekers to be a holy, sacred vortex similar to the Himalayas in Tibet. We had been drawn here. We knew we needed to let the world go for a while, and this was the perfect place to do it.

Soon into our retreat, we had an unexpected visit from several Ascended Masters, Jesus among them. We had felt these Masters before but had never experienced them with such presence. They told us we had some very important work to do during this month and that they were here to guide and support us. We welcomed them all with open hearts and felt blessed to have them with us.

It soon became obvious that they had some serious plans for us. Jesus, in particular, was leading the way and it wasn't long before we found out why.

One day, as we were sitting in meditation, we suddenly found ourselves lifted back in time two thousand years. We had had no previous warning about this and it had been the furthest thing from our minds. But, suddenly, we were reliving our lifetime with Jesus. It was so real and intense. Out of this experience came the most dynamic clearing of energy and emotions either one of us has ever known. With the clearing came an opening of our hearts and a blossoming of our love that was indescribable. It changed our lives forever.

For several days afterwards, we just looked at each other, stunned. What had happened here? Who would have thought that we would be traveling back two thousand years to clear up some old and frozen pain that *we didn't even know we had in us!* Jesus explained that many people on our planet have pain frozen inside themselves about him. He spoke to us of the antiquated belief systems we have held from long ago about being suffering, sinning and unworthy people. He showed us that we have been conditioned to deny and hide our "Christedness" and that this has caused us to live in repression of our true power.

He showed us many things that day and many more in the days to follow. He was intent upon clearing out old energy, old and encrusted misconceptions. And we agreed with him on all of it because we knew that he was right. We could feel it inside ourselves. We knew that if we didn't honor this energy that so desperately needed clearing, we were going to be hampered by it. And we didn't want this. We wanted to move forward—with all our hearts and souls.

Since our time with Jesus in that little cabin on the mountain, we have explored what we experienced and what he said in great depth. We have looked inside ourselves, we have facilitated other people, we have explored the energy thoroughly. And we have reached some startling conclusions. We have concluded that many of us are stuck in exactly the same behavior and thought patterns that were established in us two thousand years ago!

We, as a western civilization, cannot move forward until we explore, unravel and heal our pain about Jesus. Until we do this we are frozen in place, living by thought patterns that are outdated and inappropriate. Until we identify and clear these patterns, we cannot establish new ones that are in alignment with our true natures. We need to transform these old patterns so we can be free.

The freedom of our expression of goodness and God-ness has been thwarted by our ancient belief systems. True, there is value in what we have learned from our past, but there is little value in being stuck there. Our past was our present teaching us, not trying to hold us back. As we live in these times of greater spiritual awareness, the need to reevaluate ourselves becomes critical.

Jesus was an extraordinary man. He has been by far the most influential figure upon western civilization in the past two thousand years. There have been many other great teachers, but none have left such a wide and blazing trail of love and tears in their wake. All that is carried out in his name, both positive and negative, was born out of his lifetime. He rocked this Earth in so many ways.

Think about it for a moment. How has his life affected you? Even if you are not Christian, do you feel his impact upon your life? We believe that everyone has felt the impact of this man, directly or indirectly, for his life was instrumental in shaping the subsequent spiritual, social, moral and political structures of our western world. It has molded us on many levels.

The intention of this book is not to address the issues surrounding Jesus, but to delve directly into the heart of what this man meant to us inside—person to person, soul to soul. His teachings inspired us to see God in ourselves. In retrieving what he symbolizes and represents to us, we can better understand our dance with our spirit—our relationship to our God-Being. But before we do this, we must clear all the confusion that stands in the way.

Jesus was considered a revolutionary. He was a God-directed, outspoken, passionate and compassionate man. He was a great visionary. He saw the power of love in each of us, and this was his focus. He set our hearts aflame by loving us and believing in us. He told us that we needed to change how we think of ourselves, that we needed to know ourselves as empowered, conscious Beings, responsible for shaping our lives and the lives of our children. He told us that we were Beings of love and compassion, and that we were worthy and divine.

How is this any different from what we are saying to ourselves two thousand years later? He *knew* it to be true. The question is, do we? And if we do, are we living it fully?

Many of us find ourselves governed by messages and conditioning that run counter to what Jesus taught. Ironically, all of this conditioning has been done in his name. This is one of the primary reasons why there is so much conflict and confusion associated with him.

Think about it for a moment. In the name of Jesus, what patterns run you? What are some of the messages that come instantly to your mind when you think of religion, of worthiness, of freedom? Here are some examples that illustrate how powerful the destructive messages can be. We realize there are also many constructive messages, but here we wish to emphasize those that have blocked our spiritual freedom.

- I am a sinner.
- I am unworthy.
- I am guilty.
- I must pay for my sins.
- I must never think of myself as being Masterful—it is sacrilegious.
- Poverty is noble.
- I must give but not receive.
- Suffering is a sign of Godliness.
- I am a sinner, therefore I will never be good enough.
- Just by virtue of being born, I am a sinner. I am condemned for life.
- I must judge myself harshly because I am such a sinner.
- God will punish me.
- I must punish myself.
- Self-flagellation is good. It is a sign of holiness and purity. It makes me worthy.
- The more I beat myself, the better I am.
- Sex is shameful.
- I will never be worthy of heaven.
- Jesus died because I was so bad. I am reminded of this every time I see a cross. I have to pay for this.
- I am so bad that Jesus was inhumanely tortured on account of my badness. It's my fault that he died. I am to blame.
- He died so that I could live—so that I could keep on being a suffering sinner.
- I am unforgivable.
- I am going to hell unless I'm really good and beat myself really hard. I have to pay, one way or another, to get into heaven.

- I must prove that I am worthy, that I am good enough.
- God loved Jesus so much that he put him on the cross, tortured and killed him. He was his son and this was a loving thing to do because of my sins. Jesus was God's ONLY son!
- He was the one and only son that God killed because he loved him so much.
- God is a man who sits on a throne watching me. Watching all of us.
- God is to be feared. If I am not good, He will decree that I will burn in hell forever.
- I am beyond redemption.

The list goes on and on. Think about it for a minute. Do any of these statements ring a bell inside of you? Have they influenced you? Do any of them leave you feeling confused, conflicted, angry, intimidated, untrusting? How many of these messages have been a part of your conditioning? You may have thought you had moved beyond this, but how much of it is still affecting you and how you feel about yourself?

Examining this is important for it reveals how we have held ourselves back in his name. What a paradox! No wonder there is so much separation, confusion, pain and resentment around Jesus. It's completely understandable that we would want to disassociate ourselves from him.

Many of us have thrown out the thought of wanting a connection with him. Unfortunately, we have "thrown out the baby with the bath water!" Truth be told, we have a deep, deep love and connection with this Master Jesus and all the goodness he represents. In opening to this connection, we open ourselves to the depths of our own goodness. Those dusty, cobweb-filled corners within us are brought to light, and we find the spark of passion for life that we have missed since he left us two thousand years ago.

His original words, his original sacredness, his original inspiration lives on inside of us all. It lives on, safe and intact, in the core of our hearts. We have protected it well, as it is most precious to us.

We are his brothers and sisters of heart who have come here to re-ignite these beautiful and sacred energies. We are ourselves revolutionaries. Because times are different now, we can express ourselves differently and more openly. The truth is this: we are here to make change; we are here to express light; we are here to live consciously and with reverence for ourselves, each other and our planet. *We are here to make a difference.*

Who was this man Jesus? He represented everything good in the world. He represented truth, love, peace, healing, harmony, compassion, gentleness, strength—God embodied in man. He was a common man, living among the common people. His teachings addressed the fundamental issues that were, and remain, important to us and our well-being. His message was a message of love.

What we have seen, both in ourselves and through our clearing work with others, is that it is necessary to return to the original space of two thousand years ago to literally reconstruct the events within our psyches and resurrect ourselves. This is a cleansing that is all about *restoring ourselves to LOVE.* Without it, we remain fragmented, with parts of ourselves deeply entrenched in self-denial, resentment and conflict. We are buried under the persisting weight of old baggage. This weight greatly affects our hearts and our capacity to know our own "Christedness."

As you will see, people of varying belief systems are in need of this clearing. It does not seem to matter whether or not one is raised Christian. There is an etheric energy that has affected most everyone. The events surrounding Jesus and his seeding were far-reaching and have influenced all of humanity.

A surge of material has been written about Mary in the past five years. Much of this contains magnificent pearls of wisdom brought through various gifted seers. People have been hungry to re-connect deeply with Mary's vibration within themselves, and this has proven to be very heart-opening. Embracing Mary—and the feminine power—has been critically important. But let us remember that Mary was the Mother of Jesus, and so naturally, Jesus cannot be ignored. He is a vital part of Mary's message. To ignore Jesus and simply devote oneself to Mary, void of Jesus, is like loving your own body but neglecting your arms. Mary and Jesus are deeply intertwined. For wholeness to happen within each of us, both energies need to be restored in a balanced and loving way. This is also part of that for which Mary has been paving the way. *The time for this has now come.*

Our purpose in writing this book is to bring us together as a family of humanity. Our message is a message of love. It is not our intent to condemn or judge anything about religion or anyone's preferred path of worship or spirituality. Our intention is not to divide, but to *unite* us at our core. It is to restore the glorious depth of love within our hearts. In our experience, Jesus provides a most valuable "missing link."

As we move into our depth of love for him, we will encounter our pain of loss and separation from him. We will encounter the patterns of persecution and suffering that we took on from witnessing his crucifixion. In moving *through* that pain, we will find we misunderstood the events that took place at that time. As we explore it all from our present level of consciousness, we will be able to see the perfection of it this time and bring it to a place of peace within ourselves.

Through this restoration, we come back to our Self. We re-ignite our Christ Consciousness and enable the magnificent expression of this creative force to flourish passionately through us all. Then we can create new patterns based on love, joy and mastery.

This book is a journey. The first half is a clearing process of the old, and the second half is a birthing of the new. We encourage you to see it through to the end.

Sit back ... close your eyes ... take a deep breath ... and imagine.

Imagine yourself in a time two thousand years ago. Imagine that you have just heard of a man named Jesus. What you have heard has piqued your interest and curiosity.

You hear that he is coming to your village. You await his arrival with great anticipation. You feel an inner stirring that you can't completely explain.

He arrives. You see him and he sees you. He looks at you and you feel as if he has opened the gates in your heart. You feel that he knows you throughout. You are rocked inside with his love, compassion and God-presence. You are touched to your core.

The gentleness in his eyes and his peaceful demeanor envelope you. They move you so because you also see and feel his amazing strength—his complete dedication and clarity of purpose. Being with him is like finally coming home.

You cannot get enough of this man—his energy as well as his teachings. Life has taken on a whole new meaning for you. You join with him and his extended family. It is a joyous reunion. Your passion is ignited and you feel alive—more alive than ever before.

Life moves along in a fluid, joy-filled manner. It seems too good to be true, but you know it is real. You feel free inside.

And then imagine that one day, this man Jesus is suddenly taken out of your life. He is taken prisoner by the governing authorities. He is tried. He is convicted. He is crucified. He is gone.

Jesus is gone from your life forever.

Or so it seems.

How do you feel now? Where are you now? Who are you now?

Imagine ….

Chapter Two

 ## Mount Shasta Beckons

It is 1991, and we are on our way from Sacramento, California, where we have been living for the past year, to Mount Shasta which is 50 miles south of the Oregon border. We have driven up Interstate 5, north of Redding, and round the corner where the twin peaks of Mount Shasta loom large and majestic in the distance. She is like a giant white crystal emerging out of the earth. Upon seeing her, we immediately both burst into tears! There is such a deep feeling of "having come home."

In that moment we are visited by a clear welcoming presence who is obviously connected to the mountain. We are very touched by him and feel his desire to guide and nurture us in the days ahead. We know that this moment is a turning point in our lives. It is as though a "green light" has been activated in us, a signal that we will be living and expressing our freedom in ways beyond anything we have known before. It is time. We are ready. And God knows it.

As we neared the town of Mount Shasta, we talked about how this feeling of activation felt familiar to us. We had experienced these pivotal moments before, and each one had catapulted us into a stunning new reality that had completely altered the direction of our lives. We had learned through our experiences that the key to transitioning through these doorways was to let go and give free rein to what God had in store for us. We knew that we had no basis from which to project what was ahead for us and that we could only be open and available in the moment to the forces that would direct us.

As we sank into our trust of this new adventure ahead of us, we reminisced about times past when we had walked through an "unknown doorway." Six years earlier, we had both literally walked out of our established lives to be together. Not only did that experience feel like going into the unknown, but also like taking a leap off a towering cliff as well! Our love for one another was too powerful to deny and it was like the mysterious call of some long ago unfinished dream that compelled us both to leave our already meaningful lives to follow this deeper call of our spirits. In listening to our hearts this way we embarked upon a journey of love greater than we had ever imagined. We realized that in "jumping off the cliff" and taking that leap of absolute faith in what we knew was so intrinsically necessary to our well-being, that we had expanded ourselves and our capacity to receive God.

With our seemingly new, yet ancient love burgeoning inside of us now, we forged a path of spirit that involved all aspects of our lives—career and personal. We put spirit ahead of everything. From this time on, no matter what we were doing or what our work together was asking of us, we always felt God saying to us:

> "Put your love for Me, for yourselves and for each other ahead of everything. Put it ahead of your business and all the work you do with others. Keep love always as the flame which leads you everywhere you go."

In hindsight, we have seen that it was precisely this wisdom that has fostered the brilliance of light and the foundation of strength that has supported our every move. Indeed, we feel it has been this receptivity and devotion to love and spirit that enabled Jesus to enter our lives with the purpose he had in mind for us.

We reflected on another "activation moment" in our lives just a year prior when we had been in Hawaii attending a seminar focused on "the art of letting go." After this ten day intensive, we returned to our house in Virginia realizing instantly that we couldn't live there anymore and that our inner guidance was calling us to move to the West Coast immediately. The impulse was so strong for us to let go of everything and head westward that we did precisely that. We detached from all of our material possessions, the house and all its contents, and moved to California with plans to move to Hawaii once our Virginia property sold. No sooner had we arrived at a friend's house in Sacramento, where we had only intended to spend a few weeks, when our work took off like fire. We were so busy that we ended up staying a year!

Eventually, our plans for Hawaii dissolved as our Virginia property didn't sell and Mount Shasta beckoned. What we thought of as "our plan" was eliminated in light of God's plan. We followed the energy within which called for change and we let our path unfold— not being rigid about having it our way. As we spoke of those times past in the car that day, we felt both the exhilaration of knowing that a new horizon was rushing toward us, as well as the deep peace that comes when we surrender to the hand of God that has asked that we trust enough to follow without question.

This was the first of several visits to Mount Shasta, each one giving us the next piece to this "journey." We were soon prompted to move to Mount Shasta and were led to our little cabin mentioned earlier. We were ecstatic at the thought of living there and were pinching ourselves at how things were falling into place so beautifully.

While still in Sacramento, and shortly after we had made arrangements to rent the cabin, we had received a phone call from a previously contacted realtor. He told us about a beautiful place for rent that he thought we would want to look at. We informed him we had just found a place for ourselves and that we weren't interested. He persisted, saying he thought we should at least take a look at it. We finally agreed, as he had been most helpful earlier on.

This home, located on twenty secluded acres with a year-round running stream, was very large, with gorgeous views of Mount Shasta and the mountains north into Oregon. As soon as we entered the house, we both looked at each other, stunned, because we knew this was to be our workshop/retreat center. We didn't think we wanted the added responsibility of running a retreat center, as we had been conducting spiritual development workshops and intensives for years, and we liked using other available workshop spaces. But it was crystal clear there was a plan and it was beyond what we wanted.

As we looked around the house and property, we could feel many masters and angelic presences there urging us on and even being amused at our own surprise over this turn of events. It really seemed as though the joke was on us! All we wanted was to stay up in our little cabin and simplify our lives and here was this huge commitment that was asking to be brought into our equation. With the goose bumps of confirmation that were tingling up and down our spines, it was all too obvious that there was a greater plan than we would have consciously chosen at work here. Once again, we took in a deep breath and knew we just had to let go and allow everything to unfold.

In making arrangements with the realtor and the owner of the property, we were very specific about our intentions. We told them we would be having weekend intensives as well as people staying with us for periods of time. We said to ourselves, "Okay, this will be the true test. If we're supposed to have this place, the owner will have no problem with our plans."

The owner's response blew our minds. Not only did he have no problem with our plans, but he was thrilled about what we were going to do! He told us he had always envisioned this property being used in this way. We threw up our hands and said, "Okay, God, you win!" Ironically, after we opened the retreat center, some local acquaintances visited us and asked us how we had found the place. They told us they had been looking for a retreat house like this for years! We responded by saying, "The place found us!"

Finally, with all the arrangements made, we went to our cabin, emptied our minds and went into retreat for a month. We knew that the details of the plan for the bigger house would show themselves later. We had trusted and acted on our guidance and, as a result, things were moving effortlessly into place.

Once into our retreat, we fell completely in love with our little "sacred hideaway." We nestled in our one-room cabin on Mount Shasta with no electricity or steadily running water. We were able to pump water when we needed it by running a gas generator. We had a wood stove for heat and gas for cooking on our little two-burner stove. Everything was "back to basics," and we were both amused and relieved at the beautiful simplicity of it all.

In front of us was a range of mountains that rose up to 9,000 feet. Behind us soared Mount Shasta, visible in all its glory from our lofted bedroom. Mount Shasta, an illuminated mountain, was breathtaking, rising up to over 14,000 feet and usually snow-capped throughout the year. The town of Mount Shasta sat at her base at 3,500 feet, so the mountain's rise of over 10,000 feet above the town was very dramatic. Our cabin's elevation was approximately 5,000 feet.

Often we would look out from our front deck at the view of the mountain ranges below us glistening white in the afternoon sun. We felt above the world up here and often experienced ourselves being momentarily transported back to lifetimes spent in the Himalayas. Even though neither of us had ever been to the Himalayas in our current lives, we both experienced Shasta as having the same qualities of light and mystery that we'd seen in pictures of the Himalayan mountains. We both sensed the many dimensions of life pulsating here and it was as though we had walked into a vibrant, multi-layered painting that had enfolded us into its secret sounds and inner caverns of hidden knowledge. The power of this mountain had reeled us in and we were now its worshipers.

We had often heard of Mount Shasta referred to as an "inter-dimensional doorway," and now we were feeling the sensations of this movement pulsating through us. Sometimes it was like a quiet reverberation humming inside, making us feel serene and deeply peaceful. At other times it was like being plugged into an intense, high-voltage energy network which left us feeling dazed and breathless! Either way, we knew there was an enormous amount of inter-dimensional activity in this place, and we were becoming a part of the power of it all. We both felt strongly that this doorway would lead us more fully to our greater selves. We felt like we were in heaven.

Our days soon began to be fluid and timeless. It was exactly how you know it can be when, internally and externally, you've let go of everything connected with the outside world. Our only focus was our spirits—feeding them from within—and sharing our love and experiences with each other. We moved into an existence all our very own.

Even though we had lived according to our spirit for some time, now we understood that we had just barely tapped the surface. We were seeing it all from a new level. We hadn't realized just how truly hungry we were for the direct experience of placing all of our energy and focus exclusively upon this. This gave rise to long buried feelings of isolation and anguish over how much we had missed this connectedness in the past. We were relieved to experience our tremendous yearning for God. Acknowledging its depth felt as though it was putting the grand puzzle of our lives onto its correct axis. We were beginning to understand our true needs better than ever before.

The many days and hours at the cabin were filled with long talks, meditation, reflection, quiet hikes in the woods around the cabin, endless moments of just gazing in wonder at the beauty all around that was offering itself so generously to us. The air was clean and crisp, and we breathed it deeply as though we could never get enough. The energy here felt so pure and clean—it was refreshing to feel ourselves out of the loop of the media and electrical stimulation, and far above the confusion of mass consciousness.

We spent a good deal of time outdoors and when we walked in the woods, we could feel the crunch of pine needles under our feet and smell the sap oozing out of the bark. On the surface everything appeared quiet and still, yet underneath it was obvious that life around us was teeming with joyful purpose. We felt nature spirits abounding and we were acutely aware that they, too, were supporting us in this awakening journey.

Our ever increasing sensitivity to energy over the years had enabled us to commune with the devas and nature intelligences, and here on the mountain we felt their encouraging energies saying to us:

> "Be strong and stay open. There is great magic here for you and we are with you!"

We felt like we had many friends here on the subtle levels, and it was both very exciting and comforting for us. We soon discovered that we managed very well in this small space of ours and that our physical needs were quite minimal. We had done an extensive amount of camping throughout the years, and this was certainly far more luxurious than any camping we knew. Although it would have been spectacular to sleep out beneath the stars, we were grateful now for the roof over our heads as it was very cold after the sun went down, and the warmth from our wood stove was welcoming and cozy.

We also found ourselves not needing to eat very much, and we appreciated how we had cleansed and purified our bodies over the past year. In feeling our physical lightness here on the mountain, we knew the many months in Sacramento spent deliberately refining our diets and taking care to build our nutritional fortitude was now paying off. At the time we had been drawn to do it for our health and well-being but it was clear to us now that it was a deliberate and important part of the preparation phase for this retreat experience. It enabled us to be more finely receptive on the physical level which only enhanced our abilities to receive information on the subtle levels.

Soon after we were settled, the silence around us began to permeate our psyches. We felt ourselves unfolding like flowers to the sun, and we started to sense the presence of Masters with us. The more quiet we became, the more clearly we could hear, feel, see them and even smell some of their exotic spiritual fragrances. A mixture of jasmine and rose was particularly noticeable at times. The Masters Yogananda and Babaji were most often present in these first days. Their loving and supportive energies just seemed to waft and mingle with ours until we felt as though we were inside a warm, golden melting pot and we were being stirred like vegetables in a stew. Every day we became more flavorful and more complex in our own subtleties.

We felt ourselves growing more and more receptive and the many worlds that we were sensing began to merge as one magnificent design. At this point we felt ourselves letting go of our hold on our structured identities and we discovered a deeper contentment in surrendering to the spiritual intelligence and simplicity that had taken over our lives. There was a great peace beginning to emerge in us.

When we had reached a point of feeling pliant and serene, Master Saint Germain came to us. It felt like he had "blown in on the wind" and he was suddenly just there. His presence was warm, vibrant and electric.

He greeted us saying:

"You have come here to rediscover your own seeds of love and devotion to that which is of the highest in you. You have made this the most important thing in your life. Therefore, you are now consciously unfolding and receiving your most sacred selves. I am here to guide and direct you on your journey at this time.

"Now is a time of quiet reflection for you both—a quiet time of love and gentleness spent with us, with your own souls, with the gifts of Nature. The divine beauty that Nature provides is here to inspire you and show you the vast creativity of your own Being. Drink in the power and beauty that you see around you. It is the mirror of your own beauty and the Earth's way of gifting it back into your awakening hearts. Accept and receive. Now is your time of revelation."

During the course of the ensuing days, we grew much closer with Saint Germain and felt very much at ease with him. It felt like everything within us was being speeded up by his vibration. Sometimes he was very soft and gentle, finding his way into our hearts and minds through tenderness and understanding, while at other times he could be fiery, direct and insistent in his requests that we trust and surrender to the openings that were occurring. We felt his clarity and determination to help us in discovering ourselves and we were very grateful to him for his persistence. He continually urged us forward, saying:

"Let go, let go, let go. Only then can the true magic happen. Love everything you feel. Allow your hearts total freedom."

Frequently, we would feel ourselves being transported into the center of the mountain. The beauty and the energy of some of these inner temples were extraordinary. Shimmering light and color radiated within these sacred spaces and infused us with strength, lifting our awareness to bold new heights of expansiveness and possibility. We shed all density and became vibrating light, still conscious of our form as humans.

Saint Germain would often take us to one of the inner mountain chambers that was lit up with golden light. At first, we thought the gold had to do with abundance, but he said to us:

"This golden vibration acts as an energy conductor allowing me to open you and your systems to become more refined and receptive to the higher frequencies. This energy work I am doing is critical for both of you to prepare you for the work ahead. We will not speak of what that is at this time. It is only important that you relax in here and trust me to do my work with you. I am preparing you for even deeper levels of partnership with us."

As our work with Saint Germain progressed, we experienced a range of sensations as he moved in and through our various chakra centers. Some of the sensations were pleasant and soothing, while others were uprooting and clearing. At times he would use beautiful gems to pulsate different frequency sound vibrations through us, often leaving us amazed at how lit up we were.

After our sessions with him, we often needed to sleep for short periods. We recognized that the work being done on us was intense and our physical systems needed time to adjust and assimilate it all. Amazingly enough, we felt quite balanced throughout all of this. Our physical, mental and emotional systems seemed to be able to accommodate everything that was happening very well, and we didn't feel much of the agitation that can so often accompany major expansion experiences.

In hindsight, it was obvious that Saint Germain was clearing us and preparing us for Jesus, who made his presence known to us about halfway through our time at the cabin. His purpose and presence will be described at length throughout this book, but for now, suffice it to say that he was beautiful. He penetrated our Beings like the underground waters flowing eternally through the Earth; his love was deep, his compassion ever present, his humility awe-inspiring. We knew the key to experiencing him fully, and experiencing the freedom in ourselves, was to surrender and yield as Saint Germain had already taught us to do. We gave our hearts to Jesus and in doing so, we found our own.

Throughout our work with Jesus, Saint Germain stayed with us like a supportive rock and stabilizer. When we had questions, he helped us put the pieces of the puzzle together. When we felt over-whelmed, he would tell us to leave it with him and go for a walk. By the time we would get back, we always felt much better.

Mary was there also. Although she stayed mostly in the back-ground, occasionally we would hear her singing to us and her songs were like lullabies that soothed our souls. Her nurturing love and comfort were all-pervasive, and she said to us:

> "Even though I am not actively in the forefront with you now, know that I am here. My love with you and for you is ever present. Take my song into your heart and let me soothe you always."

During our time at the cabin, we began to see how these three Beings worked so well together with us. Master Saint Germain was the one who prepared and stabilized us, Mary nurtured us, and Jesus was birthing us. And our role in it all? To relax, trust, surren-der, allow and embrace. We knew that in surrendering to them, we were also surrendering to the Master within ourselves.

We were very grateful that we could talk to each other and bounce things off of one another. If we hadn't, we might have won-dered, How much of this are we making up? Is this for real? We might have wondered if we could really trust what was happening here. But with the two of us involved, we could confirm each other's experiences and add our own insights. Our "extraordinary reality" was not to be denied. We encouraged each other to keep opening and discovering, and comforted each other in our tears both of joy at our discoveries and sadness at our revelations of pain.

We saw each other changing as the days went by. We each watched as the other lightened, softened and strengthened inside. Our love for one another deepened, and we became closer than we had ever been even in our closest moments. We seemed to be merg-ing more fully as one—to the extent that, when we were uniting with ourselves, we were united equally with each other. There seemed to be no end to our capacity to love and be loved. This is what life is all about, we thought to ourselves. This is what is mean-ingful to us. Everything from now on must be an extension of this depth of meaningfulness.

One day, both Jesus and Saint Germain came to us and their voices joined as they said:

"You have been thoroughly prepared now to uncover some very important pieces of your etheric bodies, links to your past and to your future. As we guide you on this next phase of your journey, there will be many angels and masters with you to ease your expansion and transition into your higher frequencies. Rejoice as what you discover brings you great love and freedom."

With this message, our thoughts and inner vision cleared as though the trees in the forest had parted to show us a new path. We looked at one another and in each other's eyes saw eagerness, alertness and, indeed, readiness for whatever was to come next. Our preparation for this level was complete.

In the following pages, we give you our own individual stories. We share with you some of our own personal background, what led us to our experiences at the cabin and how we came to meet Jesus in his purpose with us.

Chapter Three

Our Personal Journeys

JACK'S STORY

While we were still living in Sacramento, we would frequently visit Mount Shasta. It was during one of those visits, prior to our retreat at the cabin, that Master Jesus appeared to me.

It was unusually warm for February and we had decided to go camping for a week at a beautiful spot on a lake, with the mountain in full view. I was having my usual morning meditation outside when Master Jesus suddenly appeared within my inner vision. His presence was so strong that it took my breath away. I was overcome with emotion upon feeling him so deeply. My heart burst open with a flood of love for him that I did not know was there. I felt humbled in his presence. I was so taken by surprise that, for a split second, I detached and just observed the reaction I was having because it all seemed so unlikely to me. Yet, I could not stop the feelings, and did not want to stop them. I knew this man to be my Master and my love was dictating my actions.

I looked up and found his eyes. The gentleness of his love was like a fountain flooding through my heart and soul at that very moment. It was as if I were suspended in time and nothing else existed for me. It was just he and myself together. He said to me:

> "I am with you, my brother. And yes, brothers we are and have been for eons. I will be close by your side from now on. Do not be confused by what is happening. There is nothing for you to figure out or fear."

I wondered how all of this was going to "fit into my life." I had never experienced Master Jesus like this before and didn't know what to make of it. I was afraid it meant I was to be a "born-again religious zealot." I wanted him to explain what this was all about, but he just gazed at me with his love and then quietly slipped away.

I knew then that I would never be the same again. I felt touched to the core by his presence and my joy at being reunited with him overwhelmed me. It was so positive it shook me up inside and I knew that I was being altered by it. It was one of those moments that we all experience when we know our view of reality is being shifted and there is nothing we can do about it. It was exhilarating. I felt much being stirred around inside, and I wasn't quite sure what it was all about. I would find out in the months ahead.

Immediately after this experience, I sat on a nearby rock and reflected on my earlier connections with Jesus. I had been raised in the Methodist church but had not practiced any formal religion since childhood. My mother died when I was thirteen, and I felt that both God and Jesus had abandoned me. No one could explain to me why my mother was taken away from me at such an early age. She was my connection to love and all that was good in the world. She was the "light in my life" that had suddenly been turned off forever.

In trying to deal with my confusion and the loss of my mother, I became angry and rebellious in an effort to ease my pain. This lasted for several years. At nineteen I started to find my inner peace through the study and practice of meditation, the eastern traditions, yoga and the more New Age, universal way of thinking and being. I remember deciding that the most important thing in my life was my spiritual development and my path to "enlightenment."

I recalled a very intense experience concerning Jesus when I was twenty. I was faced with being drafted into the Vietnam war and I knew in my heart that I couldn't participate. I had witnessed my brother returning mentally and emotionally wounded after serving two enlistments. He remains so to this day.

In my efforts to fail the draft physical, I went on a thirty-day fast in the hills in northern California. Just being alone in the woods for that length of time would bring about spiritual experiences for most anyone. Add fasting to this and I was most definitely moving in and out of other worlds. Around the tenth day of my fast, I vividly remember feeling so connected to all of life. I remember feeling like Jesus. It was as if I were seeing life "through his eyes"—whereupon *all* of life was connected. I felt his presence close to me, guiding me. I felt I had glimpsed what he had experienced by fasting for forty days. There was a bond between us.

Other than the experience when I was fasting, I didn't consider myself to have had much of a relationship with Jesus. My disdain for modern religion had clouded the feelings I had for him. I considered him to be a great teacher of deep love and wisdom, one of the many great teachers who had walked this planet. I was wondering what this was all about when I felt him close to me again. He said to me:

"You are not yet ready to know the answers to these questions. I assure you, it has nothing whatsoever to do with becoming a 'born-again' Christian."

With that, and a sigh of relief, I got up from my rock and went to find Deborah. After sharing my experience with her, we both intuitively knew that we would soon be moving to Mount Shasta. We knew that this was to be a home like none other we had ever had on Earth. We were excited, elated and moved by Master Jesus' energy coming into our field more strongly, as well the idea of making Mount Shasta our home. We felt privileged and honored.

During the retreat at the cabin, my feelings of deep love and connection with Master Jesus continued to gain in intensity, and one day he said:

"We are going to take a trip together."

No sooner had he spoken these words than I found myself back in another time and place. I looked down at my feet and saw that I was wearing sandals and was clad in a simple beige tunic. It was hot, dusty and dry. My throat was parched and my skin was dry and weathered from the intense rays of the sun. I looked around and saw that I was standing on the edge of a small market place with several people milling about, obviously preoccupied in taking care of their daily tasks. I knew that I was back two thousand years ago at the time of Jesus.

The air was pungent with the smell of fresh meat and spices. I saw trays of colorful vegetables lined up next to big baskets of fresh bread, the smell of which enticed my taste buds to come alive. Flies were everywhere, adding their steady buzzing to the chatter of the bargaining vendors.

I was a man of about average height and I felt my age to be around twenty-five. I lived in this small village and was a merchant dealing mostly in cloth and household goods. I had a wife and two young boys at home whom I loved very much. I was a simple, honest man living a simple, honest life.

One day, Jesus was speaking with a small group in my village. It was early on in his ministry and I knew nothing about him. I passed by his gathering on my way to my shop and found myself suddenly drawn into it. It was an inner pull unlike any I had ever experienced before. I moved closer, and when my eyes met his, I felt like I was suddenly in a pool of cool, clear water being refreshed throughout my whole person. I felt like he knew me to my core—he knew everything about me, and yet I felt no judgement from him, only love. I heard him saying:

> "Be kind to each other, be gentle and unafraid. You are all children of God, worthy of knowing your own goodness."

His words stirred a chord deep within me. I was struck mostly by the simplicity and honesty of them—qualities I had tried to foster in myself as well. I felt compelled to move closer and examine this man.

I had never before met anyone like him. He looked like an ordinary man, tall and strongly built, with large hands that looked as though they had seen their share of labor. He was clad in a robe similar to my own and he wore common sandals on his feet. It wasn't his physical appearance that made him seem unusual to me— it was something that emanated from him. He was a radiant, vibrant, shining light. He spoke in a loving, penetrating way with honest conviction and clarity beyond anything I had ever felt. I had never seen eyes that cared so much or heard a man's voice filled with such compassion and understanding. His eyes were like bottomless pools of peace, and I felt as though I could lose myself in them. The force of his love roused me as though I were waking from a deep sleep. I realized my soul had longed for this man and that I needed to be close to him.

I found myself aching to spend more and more time with him as I drank in his words and teachings. He spoke of truth, forgiveness and freedom. He wakened and impassioned those to whom he spoke. He healed those he touched. He melted the hearts of many with his love and his eternal faith in all of life.

One day he spoke directly to me and said:

"You are a passionate man. You can take this passion and use it for yourself and for others. You have been hungry to feel your heart being touched by God. Let this be so now. Know that everything in you is pure and holy. You are a sacred blessing from God."

When he spoke to me as being a servant of God, I felt as if my whole being would explode with joy. I had never considered myself to be worthy of such holiness, but now I knew that he was right. He had awakened this desire in me to serve and help others as he did. I felt so strongly that I needed now to leave my own personal life behind and take up the flame of truth and walk with him in his ministry. I grappled with my desire to do this because I also cherished my family and took my obligations to them very seriously. It was not a cavalier decision for me. I was torn inside and asked myself repeatedly, "What is the right thing to do here?"

But even in my questioning, I knew there was no recourse for me. I knew this flame of what Jesus called my "spirit" was so strong and demanding that I could do nothing but follow it now. I knew that my call to serve was where I needed to be and that this was right. I left my loved ones, thinking that I would come back on a regular basis to see them, but as time went on I saw less and less of them. I gave up everything in my life to follow Jesus and to join with the other brothers and sisters who walked with him. I knew in my heart that it was for this my soul had longed.

I felt so alive with him. My spirit was on fire with passion for all that was right about life—living fully with love, compassion and forgiveness and teaching others to do the same. As time went on, the crowds around him kept getting bigger and bigger. I could see that there were other people, like myself, who could not get enough of this man. They were so touched by his love and shining presence in the midst of their often gray lives.

But even though Jesus reached the hearts of many around us, I also saw that many were closed to him. Some found him threatening and called him another "fanatical troublemaker," while others simply couldn't relate to his teachings of love and forgiveness. They were too entrenched in looking out only for themselves.

We began to hear rumors that some of the religious leaders and the "powers that be" were expressing concern over Jesus' growing popularity. The crowds around him were getting larger and stronger, multiplying faster than the authorities could contain them. I sensed a turbulence growing all around like a storm brewing in the distance, and I felt its breath coming closer.

I began to feel afraid for Jesus and was worried about the possibility that those in power might take action on their dissent. I took it upon myself to be one of several that spoke to Jesus saying, "Master, you must be careful. We are afraid for you. We have heard that some of the religious authorities are condemning you for what you are teaching, telling us that we are God's children and have a right to be free. They are threatened by your words and there is talk that they are going to make trouble for you and us."

He just looked at me with love and understanding in his eyes, saying simply:

"Be not afraid."

And with that, he turned back to his ministry with even more passion than before.

He was undaunted by our news and carried on with his ministry as if we had never even mentioned it. Even though my own inner warnings were hardly silenced, I convinced myself that if Jesus wasn't worried, why should I be? I decided to ignore my fear of the unrest that was growing stronger, telling myself, "Whatever comes our way, Jesus can handle it." I didn't want to listen to my own uneasiness, and so I soon let myself be swept back up into Jesus' love and sense of mission, which obliterated everything else.

Suddenly, one day, Jesus was arrested. There was mass confusion around him. Before I knew what was happening, he had been tried, found guilty and sentenced to be crucified. I was stunned. We were all stunned.

We banded together and held the faith that he would get himself out of this mess. We had seen him perform miracles before, giving a blind man sight, bringing sick people back from the edge of death, even creating loaves of bread and fish out of thin air to feed hundreds. If he could do all of that, surely he would extricate himself from this grave situation. But he did not. He didn't do anything to change what was happening. I did not understand.

In my despair and confusion, I did not hear the noise in the street nearby until it was very loud and almost upon me. In a daze, I went over to investigate and my heart plummeted in horror of what I saw happening there. There was my Master Jesus laboring under the weight of a heavy wooden cross. People were packed all around him and the soldiers were pressed close in an effort to prevent anyone from touching him. I could smell the sweat from a thousand straining bodies and feel the weight of desperation pressing in on my temples.

Deep cries of anguish rent the air and I stood transfixed, watching this horror in shock and disbelief. I saw many of my fellow followers on each side of the street, watching with faces distorted in pain and mouths moving grotesquely in angry protest. Others were cheering, shouting, "Crucify the fool, yes, crucify him!" I heard their voices and felt fear rising up into my throat, tasting like bitter acid in my mouth.

I shouted out in anger to anyone who would listen, "What on Earth is happening here? What about God? Why isn't *He* doing anything about this? Why isn't *He* taking care of his Son? How can this be?" In my fury and frustration, I hurled myself into the crowd and forced my way through the guards. They whipped me harshly, but if it was painful I didn't feel it. I finally got close to Jesus and I could see his body trembling under the weight of the cross as blood oozed from his head where a crown of thorns was piercing his skin. For a moment, I looked directly into his eyes and saw his weariness and physical struggle—but I also saw his unquestioning love and shining strength pouring through. This amazed me. He seemed untouched inside by what was being done to him.

This contrast between the outer nightmare that was going on and his inner peace struck me hard. It almost took my breath away as I felt his love reaching me inside. In my own emotional turmoil, I found it confusing, and for a few seconds my steps lagged behind his. Just then the guards shoved me away, and I felt my own helplessness taking over. I was tossed and tumbled in the jumble of bodies as I looked frantically around to find my footing and do something to help Jesus. My mind was reeling in a thousand different directions about what to do, but I was just a simple man and knew I couldn't break through the soldiers again. I knew there was nothing I could do to prevent this ugly charade.

Finally, the procession reached a clearing where Jesus was to be crucified. I watched as they laid him down on the cross and nailed him to it. With each strike of the mallet to the nails, I felt my own bones being crushed as his were being pounded into the wood. As his flesh was being torn apart, so was mine. They hoisted the cross up into the air with his bleeding body upon it, and I felt my connection with my Master being ripped away as my heart broke into a million different pieces. I began to heave in anguish, believing the world was going to suck me into a darkness from which I would never return.

As I watched it all, I felt completely small and helpless. I was ashamed at my own weakness and my inability to change anything here, to save my Master from this hell. In my shame, I just stared up at him, silently begging to know "why?" In that instant, his eyes locked with mine, and I felt his love penetrating my body again, just like it always had. I heard him say:

"This is not what it appears to be. Remember your faith."

But I didn't get it. I didn't understand what he was saying. I was shattered inside. I felt like I, too, was being crucified. Slowly a blanket of rage rose up inside me and my legs began to shake with its intensity. I looked around at my brothers and sisters and saw that most of them were in shock. They looked numb inside. Many of them were silent. But all I could feel was the heat of my burning rage, and I thought I would explode.

The soldiers surrounded us and decreed that any of us who continued to be "followers of Jesus" would be taken prisoner and dealt with severely. They then left us alone as the dark night settled in. I could not bring myself to stay with my friends. I was too angry, and I did not know how to deal with the torment of what was happening. So I went off alone into the desert.

A number of days later, I returned to "civilization." Everything and everyone looked darker to me than when my Master Jesus was alive. I discovered that many of my brothers and sisters had disappeared "underground" and were secretly gathering to talk about what had happened and to decide what to do next. It was a time of intense confusion for us all. There was talk of some members actually denying that they had ever had associations with Jesus. I heard this and was shocked at their cowardice. I would not be one of them.

My anger fueled me forward and drove me to speak out at the viciousness and wrongdoing of the authorities. "You are all stupid, ignorant fools," I said. "You have killed the Son of God, you have crushed the light that was here to save your very own souls. You are blind and hard-hearted, interested only in your own gains and how you can profit from man's slavery to man!"

I was blatant in my outrage and boldly attacked both the Jewish religious leaders and the Roman government. "What you have done is a grave injustice against God. You will all rot in hell in your own lust for power and never know the light of love because you have been the ones to put it out. You are the ones who are now slaves to the darkness and you will die in the throes of your own greed." I did not care what happened to me. I could only see the strike against Life that they had made.

It was not long, of course, before the authorities arrested me and decided to make me an example of the torture and punishment they intended for anyone caught as a "follower." I was tied to a post in a public place and viciously whipped into unconsciousness by the soldiers. I was left bleeding as a feast for the buzzards. I died in the throes of agony.

Jesus met me when I left my body. I was glad, so very glad, to be with him again! The broken pieces of my shattered heart began to melt together as he touched the wounds of my memory. He explained:

"I was not a victim in my 'death.' I knew all of what was in store for me as it was part of the greater plan. I am proud of what I accomplished, and I know that I served God faithfully and strongly in my Earth mission.

"I am also proud of what you accomplished, my dear brother. We walked together in love and harmony and brotherhood. We touched many, you and I. This is not the end of our walk together. I am not 'dead' to you nor to any of my fellow brethren. Forgive those players whom you blame for my death for they were merely willing partners of God. Forgive your fellow brothers and sisters who denied their involvement with me for they were merely trying to survive the situation at hand. Most of all, forgive yourself for there was nothing you could have done to 'save me.'

"We are one in heart and soul. In time you will heal and understand more fully what I am saying. Our future together is a bright one as we will bring much light to those who so desire it."

With no further words, I felt him enfolding me in his love, once again, as my heart melted. Gently, I became conscious of my body, as Jack, back in the cabin on the mountain.

Slowly I sat up and started writing about the journey I had just taken. I was still shaking from the experience and knew that, whatever had just happened, I had been very deeply affected by it on all levels of my Being.

I felt Jesus close to me as I recorded the events and began to have several insights into how that life experience actually ran parallel to my current life. As my thoughts unfolded during the writing, I recalled the feeling of leaving everything to be with Jesus. It was the same feeling I have had in my current life whenever I have "dropped everything" to follow spirit. It made sense to me that this had its roots in my days with him.

I also realized that the anger and outrage I felt then, I have felt burning inside me each time I witness something which I perceive as running "counter to life." My rebelliousness and boldly speaking out in the name of truth is a pattern repeated in many, many lifetimes since then.

One of the deepest patterns I noted was born out of my own conclusions about what "they" did to Jesus; he was a shining example of full spirituality expressed openly in everyday reality, and look what happened to him! I concluded, therefore, that it was too dangerous to show one's light.

This pattern of believing I will be crucified (in one way or another) if I show my light has resulted in fear and difficulty about openly expressing my light in this lifetime as well. This pattern is one that I feel many of us currently face—a major reason why I am writing this book at this time of expanding consciousness. We are all being challenged to boldly let our light shine. This fear definitely holds many of us back and needs to be cleared in order for us to freely express our truth.

During those moments in the cabin when all of this was processing through my awareness, I knew that there was much more. The experience I had just had with Jesus would provide food for considerable thought and unfoldment for me in the days and years to come.

DEBORAH'S STORY

I have always loved Jesus dearly. I was raised with a fairly eclectic religious background beginning with the Episcopal Church. As a young child, I remember going to Sunday school and attending services, but it all seemed like play to me. When I was age six, we moved to Europe and for a while organized religion was nonexistent in my life.

When I was eleven, I went to a French Catholic convent in Belgium for a year. Being a boarding school, it gave me a really strong dose of Catholicism. I was the only non-Catholic student in the school and the nuns made it clear this was to be kept secret. It seemed like a "deep, dark secret." I sensed that the nuns pitied me for not being Catholic and that there was a black mark on me because I wasn't. Also, I had been banned from confession so I'm sure this made the tension even worse.

That was an interesting year for me because I didn't speak the language or know the rules of the religion. Pure survival forced me to learn both very quickly! The nuns were very strict and serious. I don't recall feeling much joy from them about God. Except for one nun, they seemed quite unhappy. I found this odd. The bright spot for me was the friends I made. Once I told my new friends the truth, they didn't give a hoot what religion I did or did not follow.

After a year, I left the convent and Catholicism with it. I was glad to move on because some of what I had experienced there had been distasteful to me, especially what went on in the classroom. We students were treated as though we were all poor, inadequate, shameful children that needed to beg for forgiveness so we wouldn't be punished just for being alive. It was mostly an unspoken message, but I found it humiliating and baffling. It made me feel as though there was never anything I could do to be good enough or to be acceptable. It was very stressful for me and I had a lot of stomach problems that year. Obviously, it was a difficult experience for me to digest! Anyway, I was certainly happy to move on and I have never looked back.

After my experience in Belgium, I asked my parents to send me back to England where I had been very happy. I didn't mind that there was an ocean between us. I just knew I felt better there than anywhere else. They complied and sent me to an English boarding school where I was later confirmed in the Church of England.

Being confirmed was an initiation into a deeper joining with God. Confirmation was a "rite of passage" in that religious denomination, and I loved it because it made me feel pure and holy and so much closer to both God and Jesus. I was given permission to reveal the depth of my reverence that I had never felt was acceptable, a reverence that ran deep in me, and it felt good to have it come so strongly to the surface of my awareness. I knew my feelings had nothing to do with the church or religion. It was simply me being honestly me.

Throughout all of my younger years, regardless of the country I was in or the religion with which I was involved, I was very aware of my mother's spiritual beliefs about the existence of "unseen" worlds and reincarnation. Even though she frequently attended services at a nearby Episcopal church, it was clear to me that she was "different." I knew she went to this church more out of duty to my father. In her heart, however, she was a Spiritualist and had been involved in the Spiritualist church since just before my birth.

The Spiritualist Church embraces reincarnation, clairvoyance, trance mediumship, spiritual healing, spiritual guides and all other aspects of spiritual development. However, back in the 1950s, members had to keep it a big secret from everyone outside that church because there was so much judgement and taboo surrounding Spiritualist practices. Nonetheless, within the bosom of our family, my mother's secret was safe, and she spoke very openly about her Master Teacher in spirit and the many wonderful Beings that were a part of her "spiritual family." Besides her teacher, there were a number of great big, gentle Native Americans who protected all of us; there were also angels and messengers, as well as doctors and healers in spirit. It was a cast of beautiful, loving, loyal characters who were as much a part of my life as my own flesh and blood.

As a young child, I vividly remember some of the simple things like the texture of soft robes, the color indigo blue and the musty fragrance that would waft through me every time my mother mentioned her teacher. I felt him very clearly and I found his wise, protective presence reassuring and soothing. I sensed how devoted my mother was to him and it was quite beautiful. His presence in her life was central. In looking back, I can see how he was sometimes a second father to me because my own father traveled extensively on business and was not home very often. All of these wonderful Beings gave me a great deal of comfort and seemed a very natural part of life.

When I was fourteen, my father's business brought us back to the States, and this was the beginning of some very difficult years for me. I had been far more European than American and was overwhelmed by culture shock when I returned here to live. This was compounded by puberty and a host of unfamiliar emotions that were rising up and transforming me from being a happy, carefree youngster to an introverted, shy and uncomfortable young woman.

I felt alienated, lost and alone. This was the beginning of my true spiritual search as my emotional pain began to add new dimensions of complexity to my life. It also motivated me to begin probing and asking questions about how I could help myself.

I decided I wanted to have a reading with the trance medium at my mother's church; and this was to be the beginning of my own personal, direct relationship with the "other side." I was then introduced to my own Master teacher and also to Master Saint Germain and several other wonderful Beings who have remained in my life to this day. I discovered I had my own "spiritual family." These Beings in spirit instantly became my friends and teachers, my guides and protectors. They were with me at all times, and I was aware of them just by turning my attention to them. I grew so close to them that I soon began to feel much more comfortable with the "other side" than with "regular people."

Throughout my teens and early twenties, years for me that were sometimes fraught with depression and a nagging sense of despair and confusion about what I was doing here on Earth, my spiritual teacher was, without question, my lifesaver. His love was in me with clarity, wisdom and guidance and he was a source of tremendous strength and comfort. There were a number of times when I would have rather died than be alive, and his presence literally sustained me here.

I clearly recall his words one day as he said:

"There is no point in you taking your life. You'll only have to come back and do it all over again!"

That piece of information, plus the fact that I was beginning to learn about "creating my own reality," had a huge impact on changing my perspective, and I became determined to somehow find my way to peace.

In my early twenties, I had begun to explore eastern religion, philosophy, meditation, yoga and transcendental meditation. It all seemed perfectly aligned and complementary to what I already believed, and it helped me considerably in learning more about managing my energies in this world. A few times I tried to follow a guru, but this just never worked out. I finally accepted that there was no one to follow but myself. There was no right or wrong about it. It was just my path.

In my late twenties, I had a startling realization about my relationship with my spiritual family. It became obvious to me that I had so completely merged with them that I had no idea who I was in the physical world without them. That realization scared me and brought me up short in myself. One could reasonably argue that because the subtle and physical dimensions are really one and the same, there was nothing wrong with this. But at that time, I didn't feel that way. My perception was that the two were fairly exclusive of one another and, because I really didn't want to be in the physical domain, it was very handy and more comfortable to stay in the subtle worlds.

If I'd continued the way I was going, my spiritual relationships might have become an *escape* from reality and responsibility rather than my *ally in living fully here*. But, at that time, I just knew I had a firm feeling inside that something about it wasn't healthy anymore—and that I had to do something. Clearly, my soul had decided the time had come for me to change the pattern.

I remember one day getting very angry with my guides—which was very uncharacteristic of me. I totally surprised myself when I heard myself screaming, "Go away! Just leave me alone! I don't know how to think for myself!"

I know that it was my anger that was enabling me to break away from them, and I also knew that they understood what was happening and had been patiently waiting for me to decide that I was strong enough "to grow up for myself."

To my absolute surprise, my separation from them was the most electrically jarring experience I had ever had. I felt as though pieces of my soul were being slowly ripped apart, and it was excruciatingly painful—emotionally, physically and psychically. Yet, at the same time, I felt such a deep current of relief and joy running through me that I knew everything was absolutely right. This was a very odd experience for me because it was such a mixture of feelings and sensations. I felt good and relieved, yet sore and angry; determined, yet sad and broken; clear, stable and whole, yet alone, confused and yearning. I had no one to explain it all to me, but somehow I knew I would be just fine.

I moved steadily forward in my intent to find out what it was like to live on Earth without constant communication with the other side and without them to help me the way they had. In hindsight, I can see that of course they were still very present with me, that it was only the *form* of our relationship that had changed, not the *content*. But at the time, I believed I was on my own and was determined to just "be me" in the three-dimensional sense of it. What a shock I experienced!

For the next three years, I walked this planet the way I imagine many people do from an energetic point of view. I had closed my "heavenly doors" and had to "stay here, be here, walk here, eat here."

What I realized right away was how incredibly dense and heavy I felt. Everything appeared gray to me, as though the sky were perpetually overcast with no sun shining. Energetically, I felt like I was always walking through thick mud. It was so slow and struggle-filled. I don't recall judging it to be "bad" or "sad." It was just the way it was. Without my usual magic and light to inspire me, my journey had become laborious and slow. It still had some magic, but it was as though the volume had been turned way down and it was hard to connect with the magic.

I managed to function quite well during that time, and my life continued on its steady course of learning and unfolding. After three years, apparently my soul was satisfied with my learning because, while in a healing session with a friend, I was shown that spiritual awareness and multi-dimensional insight were my path and my passion, and that the doorways were now open again. I heard the words:

> "Now you can walk with insight in both worlds and bring the two together as one. You have stabilized yourself and are ready to express this knowledge."

I found myself consciously reunited with my spiritual family and found that the nature of our relationship was now one of equal respect and admiration instead of a parent-child paradigm. My world was now broader than ever before and it felt really good to be "back in my spiritual groove."

Shortly thereafter, I left the field of counseling in which I had been working and moved directly into a full-time practice of facilitating others in their healing and spiritual development. Sometimes, when doing my own inner work, Jesus would appear and just be with me. He would tell me that I was on the right track and that I was finally learning for myself all that he had been teaching me thousands of years ago.

Once during a workshop, I suddenly found myself traveling to a different dimension of reality. There I saw myself standing in the middle of a beautiful, green field and all around the wildflowers were dancing in tune with the inviting breeze. I felt exhilarated and filled with life. Joy was radiating from my face and a glow of golden joy to match it began radiating forth from the center of my heart. Joy enveloped me like a golden cocoon. Suddenly, I felt heat inside me so hot that I thought I would explode in flames.

As I was thinking this, the flames suddenly turned into swirling rays of color that were reaching out, stretching to encompass and embrace all living things around me. In my reaching there was instant intimacy with all of life everywhere, simple and undemanding. I felt like I was living pure love.

I felt gloriously alive and one with life. I became aware that I was experiencing and expressing my true self—alive, confident, endlessly creative and rapturous. I began to laugh. It was a loud belly laugh of self-realization that shook all of my cells. As they jiggled back and forth like jelly inside, I was transformed into light by the sheer delight of it all.

"Where have I been all of this time?" I asked myself. As if in answer, I heard resounding laughter joining mine. I turned to see Jesus standing next to me, his face looking upward into the sun and his eyes crinkling with mirth.

Looking at him, I began to laugh harder. I saw the picture of my own limited awareness and how it had been so for centuries. He had watched me all of this time waiting for me to see the ridiculousness of my own limited convictions. It was as though he had been saying to himself, "Boy, is it going to be funny when she finds out who she really is!"

I was finally having a solid glimpse at the truth of my Being—not dense, limited and small, but fluid, glowing, eager and irrepressible. The joke had indeed been on me and, for those precious moments, I delighted in being the object of our mutual amusement. Laughing with him like this was like "eating bliss," each chuckle more delicious than the one before.

Finally when our laughter had subsided and we had caught our breath, Jesus turned to me and said:

> "You will never forget this discovery. Your unveiling will continue to be a journey of laughter and lightness. Savor who you really are and bring this into the focus of your understanding. This is what I want everyone to know about themselves—that they are joy, pure boundless joy."

With that thought, I found myself back at the workshop breathing deeply and feeling a new expansiveness deep in my heart and lungs. I felt the tingling from that experience for several days. I tended to be a more serious person then and afterwards was amazed at the pure lightness I had discovered in myself, and in Jesus also. I rejoiced in it and held it close in my heart for a long time.

When Jack and I found ourselves in Shasta many years later, the memory of that joyous experience came strongly back to me. I sensed that it had been a stepping stone directly toward where I was now and had opened the way for me to receive a lighter side of my spiritual awakening and not to take everything so seriously—even in the midst of what felt like great significance. This was a very timely reminder considering what we were about to experience.

At the cabin, Jesus' appearance to us felt like a glorious blessing. Although I had not anticipated his being there, his presence with us felt very natural. I was honored to have him as my teacher and wayshower and was eager that we make our discoveries together. I loved being his student and I completely trusted him in every way. It wasn't even anything I thought about. It simply was.

One evening, after sitting out on the front deck watching an exquisite sunset of beautiful burning reds and oranges flaming across the sky, I went inside to meditate and give thanks for another day of our heavenly solitude and sanctuary.

As I was quieting myself and sensing my own rhythm of peace, I felt Jesus gently enter my field like a steady warm glow. He touched my heart with his love and I felt myself melting into him as I so often did in his presence. His compassion and clarity shone through into my thoughts and I was aware of him asking me a direct question:

"I would like to take you on an important journey with me now. Are you willing to come?"

He reached out for my hand and as I reached to take his, I immediately felt myself spinning back through time as if in a time tunnel. I wondered where we were going and heard him tell me:

"Back to our days together two thousand years ago. Relax and receive what you will."

When we stopped, I was standing on brown dry earth with the wind blowing dust in my face. I was a woman of about twenty years, olive skinned, medium height wearing a blue robe that covered most of my body including my head. I was aware that it was protecting me from the penetrating heat of the sun as well as keeping the dust and flies out of my face. My clothing actually felt cool to my skin rather than hot and binding as one might expect. It was late afternoon and I had just been at the well fetching water for the night. While I was there, I had run into one of my friends whom I hadn't seen for some time. It felt good to just relax and chat with a kindred spirit.

We talked about a man, Jesus, who had come into our town several days earlier. From the moment we had both set eyes upon him and heard his voice ring out to a small crowd of curious townspeople, we had been entranced by the magic and magnetism of this man. We had both wondered who he was that he could move us so deeply without us even having met him personally. The impact of his energy was beyond words, beyond thinking. We attempted to analyze it but soon gave up. We concluded that he was simply someone very special.

As we sat by the well, we reminisced about our first encounter with him. He had been sitting on a rock talking quietly with a few people on the far edge of our village. He was holding hands with a very young boy who was obviously a child of one of the women present. The way the boy was looking at Jesus, one would have thought he had known him his whole life. I knew this wasn't so because I knew the woman and that this man Jesus had only just come to town.

Nonetheless, the boy was enraptured and a look of total trust and love shone in his eyes as he gazed adoringly up at him. Both my friend and I noticed this and turned to look at one another questioningly. Isn't this unusual, we thought. Then Jesus looked at me and I suddenly felt exactly as the child did.

There was only truth here between me and this man—nothing else. He did not look at me as a woman of enticement nor as an object of service or of duty. He simply saw through all that and went straight into my heart—or into my soul, if I had believed in one at that moment. His gaze opened me like a warm liquid fire and my heart began to beat with anticipation, of what, I didn't know. It felt exciting and yet made me a little uncomfortable as well, as though something beyond my grasp was happening inside.

I continued to watch, aware that I was not hearing his words as he was speaking to the group. I was instead swept into the feeling of something that was radiating from his person. It was a kind of glow like nothing I had ever seen—a soft, shimmering light that enveloped his body and radiated forth, especially from his lips as he spoke and his hands as he gestured. I felt the glow beginning to enter me, my body, as if I was a part of it, and I found myself holding my breath in wonder. It soothed me and made me feel sweet, simple and alive. It opened me somehow and I was bewildered by my experience.

I looked over at my friend and saw her looking at me with that same wonder in her eyes. What was happening to us here? In an unconscious effort to either understand the meaning of our experience or leave it behind, we both turned away from the small crowd that had gathered. In sharing with one another, we both realized there wasn't much to say that would explain how we felt. We just knew that something remarkable and indescribable was taking place and it had everything to do with this one man. Little did we know that this would be the start of a brand new life for us both.

After that hot and dusty afternoon, I sought Jesus out with determination and eagerness. Whenever I could, I took time away from my own duties at home to find him and sit at his feet with the others whose numbers were growing. I was enthralled with this man who had reached into my heart and wrapped his hand around it—and I was his. As the weeks passed, I came to know him more and more, and soon, I decided to leave my family—my two brothers and their wives and my father—and become one of his devoted followers. My family understood my need to go because they, too, had been touched by him.

We had traveled to a few other towns since then and now were back here in my hometown for a few days. As I sat with my friend at the water well, I tried to tell her how deeply touched I was by this man and how my love and affection for him had grown.

"He has changed me," I said. "He has opened my eyes and heart to the pure goodness in everyone, including myself. This is new to me and is something I've never really thought about before. His light shines and seems to make everyone else's shine, too."

She looked at me with curiosity mixed with envy, and I knew she was wishing that she, too, had the courage to follow Jesus.

I had become one of his inner circle, one of a small group of women that tended to him and to the needs of our growing family. My personal bond with Jesus had grown and now I was a dear friend to him. We often managed to speak together in the twilight hours after the end of a long, hot, full day. This was a quiet time when he could recharge himself and I would be there to listen to him or share with him or simply sit in companionable silence.

Sometimes he would talk to me about his earlier life and tell stories about when he was a young boy. He said to me one night:

"Even at a young age, I knew I was different from others around me, both young and old. It was obvious to me that I had a connection with life that most others didn't feel. I was filled with magic and wonder at the beauty I saw in the simplest of things and creatures.

"I would hear voices in the mist and see colors glowing around people of which I soon realized others had no notion. I was perplexed and wondered what was wrong with them. After a time, it dawned on me that if they had known what I had seen, they would have wondered what was wrong with me!"

His travels to the Far East were among my favorite of his stories. Endlessly curious to understand more about the great Masters who had inspired and taught him so much, I was forever fascinated by the out-of-body and "other worldly" journeys they made together. It seemed to have been a time of vast learning for him. I could easily understand how he could be so peaceful now because his experiences had taught him to be self-sufficient and completely fed by his source within rather than from anything around him. He could give because he was already so full.

His presence was mighty and strong, and it ignited my own passion and belief in myself. I began to recognize that I, too, had this inner strength growing inside. His love seemed endless, and every day I saw clearly how his "fountain of God" was always there to feed him and others through him. He performed many miracles of healing by simply laying on his hands and praying for God's love to heal the wounds and sickness there. I marveled that he never looked any different after someone had been healed, never showed any signs that he felt successful or grand because of what he had done. Quite the opposite, he was always humble and gave thanks no matter what the outcome.

His pure acceptance of life, and the way it moved, amazed me and helped me to nurture that same graciousness within myself. Being close to Jesus enabled me to be carried by his oneness with God, to learn about it and find more of it in myself as we moved about together.

I would often hear him say:

"Trust in life for it is God's will unfolding. I am not the answer, He is. Put your faith in Him and you will know you are whole."

As time went on, our group traveled to the surrounding towns and addressed many, many people. Jesus would often speak about love and forgiveness saying:

"You are beloved children of God. You are beautiful and sacred to Him. Reach into your hearts to forgive one another and let the joy of God shine through you. See the innocence in your children's eyes and let it remind you of that in yourselves which has been long forgotten—that you are love, made in love, wrapped in love forever."

He would also tend to the many who were sick and dying, bringing them hope and faith if their bodies did not heal through his touch. It seemed as though there was never a time when someone was not in need of Jesus' loving care and gentle wisdom. Only the darkness of night gave him respite, and sometimes not even then was there time for sleep as those hours were often spent in prayer. He had a purpose and a mission, and he lived it every moment.

As Jesus' ministry continued, the crowds became larger and larger. People flocked to him and couldn't seem to get enough of his wisdom and strength. One day, I happened to overhear two men talking about Jesus and was surprised to hear them say, "He's going to get into big trouble if he's not careful. Those rabbis, they don't like him. They say that he's turning people away from the sacred texts and making them believe they are better than the Elders. He'll be dealt with in a nasty way soon if he doesn't stop irritating them."

My heart began to pound in my chest as I listened to them. I asked myself whether they were telling the truth or just being evil gossip-mongers. I anxiously hurried on to find some of my friends and tell them what I had heard only to find that they had heard similar rumors from other people. We looked at one another in alarm. When we alerted Jesus that this was happening, he simply shrugged it off. We cautioned him to begin protecting himself and to minimize his public sharing. We wanted to protect him. We sensed a growing need to do so. But he would have none of it. He seemed to know something we didn't, and he told us not to worry.

He continued his work openly. I saw no fear, anger or confusion in him about the growing dissent that was rising all around us. All I saw was his peace and love for what he was doing.

One night, Jesus brought us together. We sat together as we always had and shared our loving communion with food and drink. It was a sacred moment for us and fused our energies into stronger patterns of love and devotion. This night seemed different, though. I sensed that this was the last time we would be together this way. Nothing seemed quite real, and although I opened my heart and soul to Jesus as I sat next to him, I also heard a voice of doom whispering inside of me. I didn't want to hear it. It was telling me that something was going to happen soon that would change all of this, that "the sun that warmed me was going to grow cold." My own senses scared me.

I could not bring myself to share what I was feeling with anyone around me, even though I loved these brothers and sisters with all of my heart. I was afraid that speaking about it would make it come true, even though I wasn't exactly sure what "it" might be. Instead, I began to close myself off from everyone and distanced myself even from my most Beloved Jesus. I was afraid to be alone with him—afraid to be with my feelings about what was happening. I felt myself becoming rigid as my fears began to turn into a panic.

As I looked at those around me, I realized that I wasn't the only one feeling uneasy. In the eyes of my friends I also saw a desperation rising. We were trying to be more and more careful about where we would go and where we would let the Master speak, although our efforts were of no use. He did not heed us at all, but simply went wherever he was needed.

One morning, as I was on my way back to Jesus after a night of attending to an ailing woman, several of my brothers stopped me on my path. They told me that Jesus had been arrested by the authorities and that he was going to be tried. I looked at them in horror and confusion. What on earth was happening here? This was Jesus, my Beloved Master. Why were they doing this to him? I could not understand.

In our fear and panic, we huddled together and talked wildly about what we should do. We decided that there was nothing to be done but to wait for him to do something about all this "nonsense." He was a great miracle worker—surely God would get him out of this mess.

We waited, soon hearing that he had been tried, found guilty and was to be crucified. We realized in total shock that he had done nothing to stop this gruesome chain of events. Maybe he still would. We hung onto this thought in a desperate attempt to calm ourselves, but inside we were trembling in our fear and helplessness.

Those next hours were agony, waiting, just waiting for him to come back beaming with joy as always. Time passed—and still nothing.

Suddenly we heard loud shouting from a nearby street. We all jumped up with anticipation and hurried to see if it was our Master returning to us. We arrived at the scene of all the hubbub and were stunned at what we saw.

It was not our Master returning but a huge crowd with Jesus in the middle of it, his body bloodied and bent, laboring under the weight of a big wooden cross that had been tied across his shoulders. Guards were all around, shouting and flailing their whips at anyone who tried to get close to him. I could hear the biting, slicing snap of leather as it fell across my Master's skin in their efforts to goad him on faster. I cringed at the sound and bit my tongue as I screamed in pain for him. I had to get near him and help him somehow.

I threw myself headlong into the pack of people and pushed my way closer. I could not get right next to him, but was close enough to see rivulets of blood flowing down his face from thorns on his head and the sweat pouring off his chin as he stumbled under his burden. I was desperate to help him, but it was impossible for me to get through the raging guards. What could I do? I stood helpless and dying inside.

I followed him to the hill where two other crosses were being mounted. We saw that there were two other men who were being crucified as well, and they were being lifted up into the air like human sacrifices. I saw their faces distorted in fear, their bodies straining against the nails as they cried out in their torment and pain. In between them stood Jesus, collapsing as he shed the weight of his cross.

We watched as the soldiers laid his body down upon it and began hammering the nails forcibly into his feet and palms. The sound of each pounding strike exploded in my own heart, and I put my hands up to my ears to shield me from the sound that echoed relentlessly in the darkening sky. I opened my mouth to scream, but I had no breath in me as my body doubled over in silent agony. I felt like I was being ripped apart.

They hoisted Jesus up with his cross, and I expected to hear him cry out in pain and anguish. Instead, when I looked up at him, I saw only his radiant peace and glory. He seemed to be in a very still place as though he had moved beyond the pain of his body and mind. For an instant I was mesmerized by the gracefulness of his body and the stillness that emanated from him there. It was as though he were poised on the edge of light, yet resting to give us all a chance to feel him one last time.

I knew that if I could have been close enough to see into the depths of his eyes, I would have witnessed what I always had seen there—light, serenity, and most of all, divine acceptance and love. I could feel it coursing through my body as strongly as I had felt the pain just moments earlier. His body was bleeding and pale in the shadows, but I knew in my own heart that his eyes were luminous and filled with love, just as they always were.

Suddenly I felt his presence, his energy, touch me. It was so strong that I could have sworn that he had his arms wrapped around me as if he would hold me forever. I felt his love fill my heart and heard him whisper to me:

> "Fear not my beloved sister. Fear not. It is not as it appears. I am with you now—and always."

For an instant, my heart dissolved into his—and then, suddenly, he was gone. My legs gave way and my body crumpled to the ground as I fainted into the darkness. I welcomed this abyss as it pulled me into itself, giving me brief respite from my confusion and unspeakable sorrow.

I don't know how much time passed, but I awoke to find people milling around me in what seemed like slow motion. The ground was wet and cold, and my body felt sore and empty. I saw deep wounds in the center of my palms where the blood had turned brown and sticky.

I wondered what had happened. And then it all came rushing back to me, and I remembered why I was in this place. Through dry eyes that were beyond tears, I looked up at the three crosses. In the center was my beloved Master Jesus hanging, lifeless and discarded. My heart reached out in a futile attempt to find the soul in his body, but I was met with silence and emptiness. He had gone.

The wind was howling and the sky had become as dark as night. I could make out the shapes of some of my brothers and sisters at the base of the cross, and I pulled myself up to go and sit with them. There were a few guards whispering nearby, but they left us alone with our grief and numbness. Somewhere I heard crying and moaning, but amongst us there was no sound. We were frozen, stunned, speechless—inside and out. A long time passed as we sat that way, and then the guards came and shooed us off.

I don't remember much after that. There was a time when I heard that Jesus had risen from his grave, but I was not there to see it. I knew it had happened, though, because I knew him. I was aware of his energy around me sometimes, but my sadness and loss were so great that his presence could not penetrate my numbness. When he had died on the cross, I felt that I had died with him. Now I was just an empty shell not caring about myself or anyone around me.

I went quietly crazy. Insanity was a much safer world for me. Somehow my sisters took care of me, but I didn't last very long. My life light was out and there was no point to continuing on in the body.

One day, I simply died alone in the dark.

I went straight to the light and there was Jesus smiling at me. I felt free and warm and it was wonderful to see his face alive and joyous looking at me so adoringly. "What a blessed day!" I thought to myself. "I feel whole again."

I looked at him and I looked back at the shell of my body upon the Earth. I asked him, "What happened?"

He replied:

> "Your Light came to life, but you felt that you could not hold it without me there. Now you find that it is still in you. We will grow from here, my love. We will grow from here."

Gradually, I felt my consciousness returning to me as Deborah. When I opened my eyes, I realized my face was wet with tears. For a few moments, I just listened to myself sob quietly. It felt like a great weight was lifting.

So many emotions tumbled around inside me. Slowly, I began to understand the deep ache in my heart, the ache of having missed Jesus in this way for two thousand years. Reconnecting with him so deeply on this journey was glorious. I realized that I had been secretly pining for this man, pining for his deep love and caring. Even though I had always felt his gentle presence with me, I had not felt this intensity of kinship, passion and oneness.

I began to write down all that I could remember about my journey. As I did, different thoughts and insights began to emerge. Patterns started to take shape, and I became aware of certain patterns weaving through that lifetime that I have experienced in this lifetime as well. I knew that whatever decisions I had made two thousand years ago were affecting me and my life today. The parallels were too obvious to ignore.

I joyfully acknowledged the deep love and devotion that motivated me to give up my whole life to follow and tend to Jesus at that time. It was the same feeling I have experienced regarding my love for God in my current life. A deep reverence within has always compelled me to keep my burning spirituality as the center of my existence. It is my life.

I saw the serenity in the simple giving and sharing that I experienced with the "family" of Jesus. I have always striven to have meaning in my relationships with others and with life and I am happiest when everything is simple, basic and honest.

Gradually, my thoughts turned toward Jesus' crucifixion. As I began writing down what I could remember of this, I started to tremble. Insight struck me like a bolt of lightening. I understood why I had always felt so vulnerable about "showing my light" in this world. I have done it anyway, and with increasing sustaining power as the years have gone by, but deep pain and anguish have often accompanied it. I had thought this was just my own private torment. The possibility of this pattern was not new to me, but I had never seen the connection so clearly nor felt the weight of the conclusion I had drawn while witnessing Jesus' crucifixion.

As I had watched his demise again, I had seen how I had concluded that openly expressing my Light would bring certain death in one way or another. I recalled, once again, the familiar sensation I have had in this life after having done something particularly "revealing" and feeling afterwards that I was just "waiting for them to come and take me away!" In an instant, my compassion opened to myself, and I could feel my understanding wash like healing water over all the past fear and naked vulnerability that I had known.

In looking at how I had coped with Jesus' death, I saw both my withdrawal and my "going crazy" in response to overwhelming pain as familiar. Although this has not happened in this lifetime, I have had similar experiences in other lives since Jesus. I know that during many lives, I have been called "crazy" for being a sensitive. Understanding the source of these feelings gave me tremendous compassion for both my innocence and for the depth of my love and dedication.

With all of these insights and emotions surfacing, I felt a profound cleansing taking place on all levels of my Being. Afterwards, I felt both exhausted and exhilarated.

A few days after this sacred walk into my past, I became aware that a deep love and passion had been reawakened in me. My heartache had completely lifted and had been replaced by a solid, resounding joy. I understood that two thousand years ago, Jesus had held a vital, living place in my heart which I thought had died when he was crucified. Now, I realized that he had never abandoned me, but that, in fact, *I had abandoned myself.*

In cleansing the trauma and unfreezing my emotions, my heart was opening in a new and powerful way. My love was overflowing like a beautiful fountain, and I felt whole in a way I never had before. I was deeply content and profoundly grateful. I loved being back with Jesus in this way, and, even more, I loved being back with myself. In taking this journey, I had received a great gift from my spirit.

Our month-long retreat was full of many wondrous, soulful experiences that we could never have anticipated. Toward the end, we both became aware of our deep hunger to be "of service," not just from a desire to help people or be altruistic, but from a deep dedication to God's will and to being His pure agents and servants. It was akin to what many initiates feel inspires them to give their lives to God by joining a monastery or a holy order of some kind. In our case, our "monastery" was to be out in the world. We were profoundly stirred by these feelings of devotion; they spoke to us of our yearning to surrender fully to God. We found ourselves consciously and very deliberately renouncing our own will and giving our lives over to God's will.

Deborah felt compelled to shave her head as a gesture of renouncing her physical identity and fully surrendering to God's will. She said that she "wanted to bare her crown, be naked in the eyes of God, unadorned, purified and innocent."

She felt very strongly about it and had someone in town do it for her. Jack speaks about how it was for him observing the event.

"When she first mentioned it to me, I wanted to do it with her, as well, and then when I thought about it, I decided I wanted to wait and see how it would be for her. One could say, I 'chickened out!'

"Once I saw her with her bare head, however, I found myself moved to tears by the energy of surrender and purity that she now emanated. I saw how deeply she felt about her purpose and desire to truly join with God and be an unwavering instrument of service. I saw her Godliness. Not that I hadn't seen it before whenever I looked at her but, with her head shaved, there was an absence of "image"—there was simply purity. It took me back to my lifetimes as a monk in the Tibetan mountains, and I felt the deep serenity that comes with this level of surrender to God's will. Needless to say, shortly thereafter, I was shaven-headed myself!"

In sharing this story, we emphasize that the desire to shave our heads came from deep within us. It was not just a flight of fancy or a desire to find a new identity. Rather, we were saying to the universe and God, "We renounce the material and the physical world as we have *identified* with it. We recognize that we are no longer *of* this world nor do we pretend to be. We are simply here as God's instruments and for this we are eternally grateful."

It was a simple, beautiful celebration of spirit that returned us to our naked innocence and melted us into our wholeness and divinity. We were in bliss. It was another powerful, life-shifting event. Shortly after this, Jesus and Saint Germain came to us and told us:

"Your work here is complete. It is time to go down off the mountain and share what you have learned with others. Your retreat property awaits you for its use. Your sharing of what you have learned here will not only benefit others, but it will also help you to integrate all the expansion and growth that has occurred. And do understand, there is much more ahead. Go in peace."

We closed this chapter of our lives with bittersweet feelings. It had been such a special time of simplicity, love and reunion. We had opened and blossomed in so many ways. Besides our spiritual adventures, our love for each other had deepened, and now we had this extraordinary month of magic to add to our memories. We knew this ending was just another beginning, and that our spirits were eager to soar and break new ground. Our dedication to be of service was alive and purposeful. We were strong, we were "plugged in," we were passionate and we were joy-filled. We were also like two bright, innocent children set loose in God's playground. Were we going to make mischief or magic? As it turned out, both!

Chapter Four

Project Lighthouse

Wᴇ sailed off down the mountain and did our best to readjust ourselves into the "real world" (relatively speaking). We moved into the big house we had rented prior to our time at the cabin and began working to make it into a special, sacred space where people could come to heal themselves and to do their inner clearing and restorative work. Our inner guidance told us the center was to be called "Lighthouse." It would be a two-year project.

It may sound funny, but just being in a house with electricity was an adjustment for us. We had become so used to being "off the grid" that now we were sensitized to the electrical airwaves. Being in the midst of all these electrical appliances, and even admitting that we would have a need for them, appalled us at first. It made us want to go straight back up to our cabin to get away from it all! The feeling of disorientation reminded us of times when we had camped for a week or more in the wilds and then reentered "civilization." We remembered the contrast of feeling so peaceful in the simplicity and rhythm of nature and then feeling jarred both energetically and emotionally by being back "in the world."

The demands of what we were setting up at Lighthouse forced us to adjust quickly. We had substantial work to do in order to make the house into a retreat center and we were immediately faced with consumerism—buying mattresses, bedding, linens, towels and kitchen supplies for at least fifteen people. The house could easily accommodate that many. There were moments when this seemed like a daunting task, considering that we had just been in an altered, refined state for thirty days. But, we knew we needed to accept that we were "coming off the mountain," and now our job was to put our refined energy toward positive action and manifestation.

Besides purchasing supplies, we also needed to furnish Light-house. We had wanted to keep it as simple as possible because of our slim financial resources so we got very creative. In the base-ment of the house, the owner, a building contractor, had a com-plete wood-working shop which he gave us permission to use. We say "us" liberally because Jack would be the one using it! Jack will be the first to admit he is not all that much of a handy-man, but as he says, "With the full range of tools that I had avail-able, even I could cut a board straight and piece together some simple furniture!"

So Jack built tables for dining and nightstands for the beds while Deborah sewed covers for all the foam mattresses as well as made floor pillows, curtains for the windows and other domestic projects. At times, we had our doubts about whether we were doing the right thing with this retreat center because we were extending ourselves beyond anything we had previously known. We questioned this not just in terms of our finances but also in terms of our commitment. Were we getting in over our heads? Were we taking on too much? Was this bigger than we wanted? Would we be able to pull this off? At times we still pined to be back up in our little cabin, but we knew there was a plan so we kept to the task at hand—preparing Lighthouse for its purpose.

In hindsight, it was obvious that we were facing the next level of our challenge to trust ourselves and to follow our desire to be of ser-vice. We felt a bit like butterflies emerging from a cocoon. Would we fly? We had to let go and trust what our spirits were urging us to do.

One evening, the Masters came forward and addressed us:

"There is much taking place for you here and for the many who are part of this project. It is a time for gathering your resources and holding your vision—being strong and steady, allowing never a doubt to enter your thoughts. It is a time for focusing on the whole as you understand it to be, using whatever discipline is necessary to relieve yourself of the habits of doubt which enter your minds from time to time. It is important that you wean yourselves from any "negative" thinking, and train yourselves to be constantly moving in the realms of the Light, thinking of the Light, doing of the Light, being of the Light. At first this will seem like a somewhat difficult exercise, but you will find that, with practice, it will become easy very quickly. Persevere in this until your world, as you know it from day-to-day, from moment-to-moment, is a singular one without any duality.

"The two of you do not recognize the enormous scope of your power and passion. You underestimate yourselves so much, so incredibly much. You have not grasped, to date, the expansiveness and the truth of who you already are. This is not a chastisement on our part—we are only showing you where you are. We wish to alert you to what appears to be a tremendous ignorance on your parts. It is not just an ignorance born of the mind, but truly an ignorance of the responsibility that goes hand-in-hand with discovering yourselves as Light Beings and becoming active Lightworkers. You are responsible for owning the greatness and capability of your Light.

"You constantly wonder why you have been chosen to be associated with Masters of such high quality and fiber. You have not been "chosen." You are also of that same quality and fiber. You must raise your standards of your vision of yourselves and wholeheartedly release your past perceptions of yourselves as 'smaller' than you truly are. We know that you are already in the process of doing this. However, a more determined effort is now necessary—a greater leap into your own faith is called for. You are ready for that now. You are prepared for that. It is time."

The Masters were urging us to be more disciplined in our thinking, more diligent in maintaining the greater vision of ourselves and what we were doing. They were prompting us to come into perfect alignment with our *true* selves rather than perpetuating outdated and inaccurate identities.

At first this was a stretch and we had a hard time assimilating the breadth of our Beings, which the Masters repeatedly pointed out to us. Even though we had begun to experience this as truth in the cabin, we hadn't yet translated it into our daily physical lives. "Out in the world," we were faced with the challenge of living it. With the Masters' encouragement and prompting, we began to open our minds to embrace more of an expanded view of ourselves and, as we did so, it became easier to hold our vision and focus about what we were doing.

One evening Master Saint Germain came forward to shed more light on this subject. As he spoke, he reminded us of our deep soul connection together and we felt his love touching us:

"I am beholden to you as we have journeyed together amongst the stars. I make my way here tonight as a greeting to you both and to carry the seed of Light. I bring to you, as well, the salutations of many old and near, dear friends of yours—Masters, as you would call them—who are in truth, comrades in Light. We are all equal in nature and in honor, and now you consciously take your place as one of us.

"Tonight we open a Window of Light in your body that will enable you to see more clearly and know more deeply the essence of Mastery that you are. I will touch that place within you, your inner eye, thus releasing this wisdom more fully into your conscious minds (we could feel him working in our third eye area).

"In many lifetimes, you have known a veil over this area of your magnificence—a veil which has served to keep you in your own ignorance on purpose so that you could learn the other things that are important to the expression and manifestation of your Supreme Light here on Earth. Have no fear or judgment of your character in this life, and lives past, when you have been ignorant. Instead, bless those days of darkness in the knowing that they have brought you now to the resonance of a greater Light, a greater joy and a greater knowing of God within. Now this veil lifts from you since you no longer need it—and you, as Masters, can reign."

As he worked on us, we each felt a powerful quickening of energy in our third eye that made us feel exhilarated and light. It was as if an ancient portal of understanding was being unblocked and opened, as if our sight had been set free.

We were later told that our inner vision would be much clearer now but that, for a time, we might occasionally feel a straining in our foreheads. He assured us this was nothing to be concerned about as it was simply due to the veil dissolving and the new, stronger energies emerging in that area.

We felt both elated and touched. It was such a gift for us to have this kind of assistance and we felt extremely grateful. Earlier, while at the cabin, we had realized how lost we felt for lifetimes and how we truly longed for our deep connection with God. We had also felt the sadness, despair and anguish that went along with those lost feelings. Now, sitting with Saint Germain, we both realized that none of those feelings were with us. In having the veil lifted, it was as though they had been washed away forever. A deep peace came over us.

We inhaled with deep satisfaction as we felt Saint Germain's violet warmth enveloping us and we smelled his musty, exotic perfume— the familiar mixture of jasmine and rose. We remarked to him, "Your fragrance is delightful," and he responded with:

> "It pleases me that you can smell this. It will fill the entire house—a lighthouse, indeed it is. Relax into the grace of our energy here."

As a result of our meeting with him, we found ourselves much more relaxed about the unfolding logistics of this project. We knew only too well that it was bigger than we were, and we certainly didn't want to step in and try to control it. We wanted very much to "let go and let God." The intensity of our excitement and desire to follow it through far outweighed any fears we had.

Besides taking care of the purely physical aspects of Lighthouse, we were also given detailed instructions in preparing it etherically. We were guided to set the energy grids of the house and property so that they would support and facilitate the movement the Masters had in mind. They explained:

> "Lighthouse is akin to a spiritual laboratory where people will come to clear the old and expand into their higher frequencies. It is essential that we join with the Elementals and other Nature intelligences here to form the necessary 'platform of stability' which will inspire, assist, balance and support the intensive expansion taking place here.
>
> "In our union, we can bring to you now the wisdom and clarity that will generate the momentum to activate these etheric grids. We place blessings of utmost love and integrity into this ground and into the atmosphere above it. Every person who comes here will be moved by this in the most positive of ways."

We felt a substantial shift once these grids were activated. It was as if all the energies, including ours, were lining themselves up and getting into proper balance and position. We sensed a strong pulse of steady purpose infused into Lighthouse and the twenty beautiful acres surrounding it. We knew we were part of a large "team effort" which was composed of many dimensions upon the etheric and Earth planes. However, it was too soon to know what all this was going to mean or how it was going to affect us and those who would be drawn here. But we did know that we had every reason to feel extremely excited, being "on the edge of it all." We were getting ready for action!

The Masters also encouraged us to continue strengthening our connection with them and the mountain every day by doing sessions as we had at the cabin. We were told it was essential because the etheric lines of communication between us would be enhanced and fortified. We visualized this being like a bridge between ourselves and these other worlds. We understood the need to keep this exchange of dynamic energy pulsating between us in order for our "inter-dimensional telephone lines" to stay open and increase in clarity.

To help us create the nurturing atmosphere that would support us, we set up our tent along the stream for our own quiet time. We knew that once people started coming, Lighthouse would no longer be our house but theirs. Having our own space outside and away from everyone was absolutely necessary.

We loved spending time in our tent down by the stream, listening to the water cascade down the rocks and watching the graceful panorama of light and shadow dance through the trees. This part of the property was remote from Lighthouse itself. To get to it, we had to walk down a steep incline that led us into another world. Whereas up around the house, the summer fields were dry and dusty, here it was lush and green, wet and womb-like. As it arched high over the bubbling stream, the foliage from the trees created a sensual sanctuary where we could find respite and be soothed back into our own centers.

In contrast to the acceleration and etheric stimulation of the retreat house, here we felt calm and sleepy, cleansed by God's water of life. Deer paths became our paths through the woods and many animals including deer, rabbits and squirrels abounded. Larger animals too—lynx, mountain lions, bear—shared their haven here with us. It seemed that we all came to the stream to be nourished. Life was abundant and we joined with it as we established our own hideaway.

With all of the elements of our new project finished, our preparations were almost complete. One evening, as we were sitting in the workshop room admiring the views that stretched for miles toward the Oregon mountains, Saint Germain appeared and spoke to us:

"The way is opening for many of us now to begin our next phase of activity and for you to understand more clearly your role and purpose in these plans. It is now the moment for you to unfold your spiritual knowing like the carpet that rolls out in front of you. And as you roll it out, you find yourself standing fresh and new in the Light of the day—and every day is God's day, every hour is God's hour, every night is God's night.

"Every seeker who ends up here is looking for that which you both have found. By the very grace of your Being, they will be ignited into that understanding of blessedness of God.

"We place upon you now what would be akin to a pair of spiritual wings so that you may fly freely and gain whatever perspective and understanding you need. These wings can be placed upon you only because you are already free. You have discovered the heart of God within your own heart. It is here that you now live.

"I now decree that the remainder of your days upon this planet will be days and nights of God. And that this place is a house of God and these lands are lands of God. This is the blessing that we bring to you this night."

We had never before heard him speak with quite so much intensity and gratitude. We were moved to tears as we felt the power of his joy penetrating our hearts. He continued with:

"There will be many more days to come on this Earth as you gather your strength and continue to follow, as diligently as you have, the song and the guidance of the Light which burns within you. You are never faltering, never wavering, always steadfast in your journey, in your knowing and in your love of that which is the Divine. That is how you are.

"My Beloveds, you are safe and you are sacred. Call upon your highest wisdom more frequently, even in the most seemingly mundane matters. This will bring you more closely united with that which you love and adore, the Divine in you. Peace, peace and more peace does rain upon you and this divine place of yours. It is with great joy and great love that we all wish you a very fine good evening."

With this, we felt him placing his hand on the crowns of our heads joining us even more firmly to his vibration and to the highest within ourselves. We felt strengthened and reassured by his message.

The stage was now set for our work with people to begin—we were open and available. We were instructed to announce our first Ascended Master three-and-a-half-day intensive by invitation only. We had no idea as to the content of the intensive. All we knew was that it was about connecting each participant to the Ascended Masters, the energy of Mount Shasta and their Master within. We were told that the specifics of the workshop would be given to us step-by-step once we were in it. Twelve people showed up based on our making a few phone calls. This was proving to be effortless.

The minute the workshop started, Master Jesus appeared to us and "took over." That was it. He was in charge the whole three and a half days. We were somewhat surprised because we had no inkling that this would be exclusively *his* intensive—we had thought it would involve several of the Masters. But certainly we did not argue with him! On the contrary, we were honored and inspired by his beautiful presence and steady purposefulness. Clearly, this was his show.

He directed us with clarity and precision. We felt as though we had been absorbed into his energy and we were but extensions of him—instruments of his every move and impulse. It was a glorious feeling to be in this motion with him. We felt privileged, alert and alive. From moment to moment, we felt like we were engaged in an intimate dance among the three of us as well as with everyone else in the group. We received Jesus fully, hearing his gentle voice within guiding and instructing us. We felt the strength of his passion and intensity pulsing through us, feeling his love at times so deep that it was like a rushing river that would flood our very souls. Soon it would turn into a still pond in which we could clearly see the direction he wanted us to go. His driving purpose motivated our actions and our thoughts.

During our breaks, the two of us would confer as to who had received the "instructions" for the next step of the workshop. Sometimes we would both have the information, but more often it was one and then the other, each of us being played like fine musical instruments ready and eager to burst forth into song. It brought us tremendous joy to co-create like this. It was fulfilling yet another yearning in us to dynamically bring dimensions of light together as one. We felt as though we had found a deeper link to God and Brother-Sisterhood, that we were plugged into our Source—and deeply happy inside because of it. We felt we had found our true calling, and it felt glorious to be impelled by such high energy, directed by such pure love.

We had complete trust in ourselves and in Jesus as he wove his beauty and depth through us and everyone there. He swept up the participants into his embrace and merged them into himself just as he had with us—and they, too, were soon his. Through us, he took them on a journey identical to the one on which he had taken us at the cabin—back two thousand years to make their own discoveries about themselves and the role he had played in their lives then.

He molded and shaped the energy so that they could see clearly into their depths and gain insight into their own decisions, their dreams, their longings. He enabled them to experience their shattering as he moved with deliberation into areas within them that were begging to be cleared. He set the stage for them to resurrect themselves so they could be restored to their soul's joy and freedom. He did these things and much more during these timeless three and half days.

We all realized this work was not for the faint of heart! This intensive was demanding, purifying, challenging and expanding. Everyone was being asked to roll up their sleeves and dive in deep. There was no holding back. Just as with us at the cabin, Jesus walked everyone through his or her "eye of the needle" and pulled them out the other side. It was a deeply rewarding time and everyone was on the edge of their seat waiting to see what was around the next corner. It was wild and exhilarating! No one there will ever forget it. Thus was born our first Ascended Master Intensive. (See Chapter Five for participants' stories.)

A number of days later, after we were rested, we received the following information from the Masters about this intensive with Jesus:

"For the past two thousand years, Jesus has been locked in a framework that has become too rigid to be useful. It is not appropriate to modern times or to the future. The only way that the Christ energy can emerge fully in your time is by bringing forward the Jesus capacity of two thousand years ago so that it can be cleansed and restored. This needs to be cleared in order to make way for the full Christ Consciousness to emerge into a clearer and more direct framework that meets the language of people as they are now today, this century.

"It begins with acceptance. The Christ Consciousness grace cannot be fulfilled until the historical pain that overlays it has been cleansed. Otherwise, it will be like trying to roll a wheel with one broken spoke—you'll have only a part of the wholeness. In light of this, we ask you to educate people. We ask you to help them understand that their piece of antiquity involving Jesus needs to be re-embraced because it is part of their wholeness of the Now.

"Many associate the word 'Christ' with the picture of Jesus— his suffering, their pain. This association with the word 'Christ' repels them on both subconscious and conscious levels, and keeps them separate from the true embrace of their Christ crystal.

"How then can they make their transition into wholeness? By bringing it all out into the open. You know that your purpose is to assist people to engage themselves directly with whatever aspects need to be healed within them so they can receive themselves now, openly and fully."

For the next two years, countless people came to Lighthouse to attend our intensives and work with us privately. This was a period of transformational explosion for us. What had been birthed in us at the cabin continued to grow. Our devotion to God lit up our lives and every day our conscious freedom became more and more a living reality. We were inspired and impassioned by it all, and we totally loved it. Gratitude doesn't even come close to expressing what we felt.

In the next two chapters, we relate the main "components" of this intensive, not so you will be awed by what took place but so you will open yourself to having your own experience with Jesus and the Master within you. When you read the following pages, imagine yourself there. Put any and all doubts aside. Let your heart be your guide and director of your experience. Do this and you will be in for a ride of transformation and blessedness.

Chapter Five

Participants' Stories

In our intensives, as we took more and more people back two thousand years the way Jesus had done with us at the cabin, we discovered the necessity and value of clearing this "body of stagnant energy." It didn't matter what someone's relationship with Jesus had been prior to the intensive, everyone seemed to have an important, essential experience awaiting them. New pathways of the heart were opened, and a true and abiding relationship with Self and Jesus was restored.

The participants came from a variety of backgrounds and walks of life. Prior to the workshops, they expressed different levels of relationship with Jesus, some not feeling connected with him at all. Most were raised Christian, but we had a few of the Jewish faith, and they had equally meaningful experiences.

Why were they coming to this intensive? Simply because their hearts drew them to it. No matter what level of involvement they had with Jesus, by the end of the intensive everyone had been deeply touched by him. With Jesus peacefully restored in their fabric of life, their paths had been cleared for deeper love and dignity.

The following stories may move you in a variety of ways. They may trigger your own memories and stir some deep inner feelings. You may even find yourself shocked at what you read, but don't be alarmed by this. For your own sake, simply observe your reactions and responses and remain as open as possible.

Our purpose in sharing these accounts is to open up the lines of energy inside of you about Jesus. As your own memories of your time spent with him emerge, you may find that nothing in your experience jives with what has been written so far about him and his teachings. This does not mean your experiences are not real and valid. They are. They are brought to you by your own inner spirit and are worthy of your consideration in every way. Your energy about Jesus has been bottled up for a long time, and only by reaching inside can you unravel it and find out what is really true for you.

During the course of this book, we will repeatedly ask you to put aside all you have ever learned about Jesus from sources outside of yourself. This book is a vehicle through which you can open to your own heart and find out your own truth about who this man was, how you felt about him, how you feel about him now, and how you would like to feel about him in the future. *None of it will be based on outside interpretations and records. It will be all your very own. All of your insights come from you and you alone.*

Please understand we are not attempting to rewrite history. Nor are we saying these stories are historically accurate. Again, our purpose is to free the constricted energy inside you about Jesus so that you can find your *own* truth. Some stories can be interpreted symbolically, and it will be up to you to interpret your own experience.

What follows is the result of guiding people back two thousand years to when they were with Jesus. Our agreement prior to taking this journey was that those attending be open to receive whatever information and insights their soul chooses to bring them. This kind of "time travel" is easy to do if we approach it understanding that we are not bound by time and space. We ask only that which is of the highest intent to come forward and present itself.

You will also notice that many of the participants were able to identify specific patterns that were seeded two thousand years ago and which actively influence their current lives. Some patterns are "negative" and some of them are "positive." Discovering these deeply-rooted patterns and their source provides us with invaluable information that can help us *now*. It is one of the great rewards of doing this kind of work.

We ask that you keep an open mind and remember that these are sacred memories belonging to very loving people. Realize that *any* reaction on your part indicates that something is being stirred inside. We encourage you to simply accept this and give it room to unfold. Have compassion for yourself and your feelings. Trust them. After all, *your* memories are deeply sacred as well.

SOPHIA

I was brought up Catholic until I turned away from it in my early twenties. In giving up my religion, I also lost my connection with Jesus even though a year before that I had an experience where Jesus appeared to me. It was a very powerful experience, but I didn't have any frame of reference in which to place it. I didn't feel my Catholicism could hold that kind of experience. Being with Jesus completely changed my life and made me realize that my spirituality was the most important thing to me.

When I was taken back in time, I found it difficult to fully embrace the journey because of the feelings of unworthiness and suffering I had taken on from my religious upbringing. I found myself to be a woman who was in a peripheral role as part of a loving circle of women around Jesus. We were supporting and nurturing him and doing our best to foster his message of love and compassion; we were very joyous and purposeful. While I was watching and feeling all of this, I was also aware that it seemed sacrilegious to presume that I could have played such an important part in Jesus' life. My Catholic conditioning was rearing its head!

I then flashed to the crucifixion and saw myself going into hiding because of all the persecution I witnessed against my fellow brothers and sisters. I had the whole range of emotions—fear, guilt, suffering and devastation. I decided I needed to leave the country, and I made it to the border where I died a violent death.

I was surprised to find that I still had so much conditioning—unresolved feelings of guilt, suffering and unworthiness. I had thought that, in turning away from my religion and embracing more universal, new age principles, I had cleared it all, or at least most of it. But, when faced with Jesus, it all came up and reared its head from a deeper place. It wasn't necessarily comfortable, but in embracing those parts of myself, I was able to experience him in a different way—as this wonderful Being. I was also able to experience the Christ Consciousness within me, separate from the religious tenets with which I had been raised.

This feeling of openness has remained with me and has expanded over the years. I am now able to be with him and to receive him. So much has grown within me as I have deepened. I now have access to him and the other Ascended Masters with whom he is connected. Now I have a beautiful and meaningful relationship with Jesus that has nothing to do with the Church. Getting to this place inside of myself was such an important step even though my mind went bananas. It will affect me for the rest of my life.

Melissa

Before going to your workshop, I didn't feel that I had any religious "baggage" at all. I had stopped going to church at an early age and didn't feel I had ever had much of a relationship with Jesus.

During the journey back, I looked down and saw big feet with sandals and big hairy legs! I was a man and not a woman! In previous past-life regressions, I have always been a woman.

I was a Roman soldier standing guard. They were about to bring this man Jesus through the crowd to be crucified. I didn't know much about him other than what I had heard from the other soldiers. They had all referred to him as a rabble-rouser, a revolutionary type of some sort.

They marched him up and put him on the cross. I was standing right next to the cross looking up at him and suddenly I was in awe. He never blamed anyone. He never said an angry word. He was so gentle. His eyes were so gentle and so loving. I was so surprised to feel his love, his acceptance and his lack of judgment of me and *everyone*. It was emanating from him so powerfully even while he was dying.

I suddenly found myself feeling terribly guilty about the part I was playing in this. His love touched me deep in my heart, in a part of me I was not aware of at all. I didn't know what to do with the feelings that he stirred in me. I also didn't know how to cope with my guilt. It was all too much for me. After his death, the only way I found I could deal with my feelings was to drink. I died as a drunken soldier.

In the workshop, I was the last one to share my story in the group. Everyone else had had such a wonderful experience. I wondered how come I wasn't one of those loving people who followed him. I was devastated. I felt like I was on the wrong side. I had been a soldier, the enemy.

The parallel I saw to my current lifetime was being an alcoholic. I've had a hard time dealing with my feelings and knowing what to do with them. I've used alcohol as a way to hide, and this workshop opened my heart. It wasn't necessarily what I had expected, but it definitely opened me to my feelings. And Jesus was there to love me unconditionally, which I so needed. Through his support, I was able to forgive myself for the role I played. I was actually able to see the perfection of it all.

IRIS

When I was first taken back with the group, I didn't experience anything other than my mind saying, "This is all nonsense." Afterwards, I expressed this in the group and you both offered to take me back a second time. I felt resistant, but I heard a deeper voice within me saying, "Go ahead and let go."

I did, and what a surprise I came upon! I found myself being one of two women married to Jesus. I loved him so very much and he loved me as well. Our life together was truly joyous, and I knew him in ways others didn't. He was a vibrantly joyous, passionate and sensual man and was not as solemn as he is usually portrayed. He had a wonderful sense of humor and laughed a lot. He was alive and wonderful, and full of kindness and gentleness. In him, I felt love of the purest kind because he knew God and saw God in all that existed.

He told me his time was coming. He warned me about it, but I didn't want to hear it or believe it. When he was taken, I grieved the tremendous loss I felt, but I was also grateful to have known him and been with him in the way that I had. I felt so comforted by his spirit which was constantly with me. He had always told me he would be with me, and now I knew what he meant.

Once I got over the physical loss of him, I carried on his message with my fellow friends and family until I died.

I was very hesitant to share this experience with the group in the intensive—I was afraid of being judged or condemned. On the contrary though, everyone was very accepting, loving and fascinated with my perception and experience of him. One person expressed that she felt expanded by my depiction of Jesus—especially his laughter. She had always thought of him as so serious. I now know why I could never accept such a one-sided version of him. I was brought up as a strict Mormon and I had always bristled at the way he was presented. He was always shown to be such a solemn man and my reaction was, "Hey, what about his joy?"

Perhaps my Mormon faith made it more acceptable for me to see him married not just to one woman, but two. Who knows if it is really true? I do feel that I knew him very deeply and I knew him as a very, very joyous Being.

JONATHAN

I was raised Catholic and was an altar boy. I went to an all-boys Catholic school for twelve years. I was afraid of Jesus; afraid of being punished by him. Even when I was immersed in my Catholicism, I would think to myself, "This doesn't make sense—he's supposed to be all forgiving and yet if I sin, I will be doomed to hell forever."

In my twenties, I completely turned away from all faiths. In my thirties, I started to embrace more of the universal concept of love and forgiveness, and then I could see Jesus as a role model.

When I went back during the workshop, I felt like I was more a presence than a person. I actually felt like I was him, but I didn't have the "nerve" to allow myself to go with it fully. So I imagined myself as an energy following him around. Upon sharing my experience with the group, you both gave me permission to feel what it felt like to be him. You made it okay, because in my mind it was sacrilegious to do so.

It was so great because that's the energy I feel I really am. And to admit that enabled me to *have* the Christ energy. At first it felt too bold, but then I could honestly say to myself, "This is who I am, this is who we all are."

Later on, you did take me back to that lifetime again. This time I was a man and I felt so closely connected to Jesus; it was as if we were actually brothers. Whenever I was with him, it felt like a reunion. We both knew what was going on and what was going to happen. I felt like it would have been nice if it could be avoided, but I knew it wasn't going to be.

When he was arrested and tried, I had such deep feelings of regret. When he was killed, I felt like I died with him; all the "knowing" and connection I had were gone. There was an emptiness inside that was so intense that suddenly my purpose and function were unknown. I felt no connection to God. I wandered around aimlessly, not caring about myself or my surroundings. It was so painful for me that I literally lost my mind. I became a vegetable. I wasn't able to maintain my spiritual connection at all.

After I died, I did reconnect with Jesus and there was such intense joy for me in this. His message to me was:

"It took a long time for you to rejoin with me. I'm here. You're here. We're reconnected."

So much became clear to me through this experience. I then understood much of the sadness that had been in my heart. Even though I had been successful in my life, I wasn't fulfilled in my heart because I still had that emptiness inside of missing him and, of course, myself. This connection was everything to me. Now that I am reconnected with him and the Christ Consciousness, I feel empowered.

I now feel I have the permission I need to feel and embrace this energy. The connection between Jesus and I has deepened. The voice that I am always hearing inside me is Jesus talking to me. I know I am the Christ Consciousness—as we all are.

LILY

My exposure to religion as a child was non-existent. The first time I entered a church I was fifteen. I've never felt as though I had any kind of relationship with Jesus. The only reason I did this workshop was because I was in Deborah's one-year art program and she encouraged all of us to attend. I really didn't think there was anything for me to clear or experience. Was I in for a surprise!

When I went back in time, I found myself not in the Middle East but somewhere in Europe, or perhaps India. I was a young peasant woman and I was alone. I didn't see Jesus around at all. Then I felt a presence, a warmth, permeating my heart. I knew it was Jesus. I could only see his silhouette at first, but gradually I was able to focus in on his eyes. I started sobbing because this was the man I knew intimately and loved so very deeply. We were lovers and best friends. In him, I knew joy, purity of soul, strength, wisdom, gentleness, tenderness, love and most of all, God.

He told me he had to go back to his homeland, and he insisted that I stay and not go with him. I begged him but he refused to take me with him. I could not comprehend this. I felt rejected, unworthy, deeply abandoned and alone.

When he was leaving me, all I could see were his eyes. The pain of separation was too much for me. I bowed my head in utter despair, seeing only his feet. As I watched those feet walk away from me, I was desolate.

After he had gone, the next image that I saw was of me looking blankly out of a stained-glass window. I had completely withdrawn and shut down. I refused to eat or drink. I just sat, frozen in place, waiting to die. Eventually I collapsed, and someone came to take me away. Soon I died, numb and empty.

As I shared my experience with the group, I began to slowly grasp why he had not taken me with him back to his homeland. I saw clearly his desire to protect me from seeing what he knew was going to happen there. I also recognized, all too clearly, a deeply-seated pattern of love linked with abandonment that I had been holding inside since that time.

I saw the correlation to my current lifetime. My father had left my mother when I was six months old. When I was nine, my mother died after having been seriously ill for a number of years.

I realized the details of my lifetime with Jesus weren't what was important. What mattered was that he was revealing a wound within me that was calling to be healed. In the face of his love, I could do nothing but surrender.

In my meditations since the workshop, I have experienced a great deal of healing with him and his presence has been a very vital, loving force. I have also found that, when I am doing healing work on others, he comes in very strongly. When he does, I just smile to myself because I realize he has been with me all along. He is family. I just didn't know it.

Regarding my issues of abandonment, I don't view these issues in terms of my parents anymore. I acknowledge they are issues within me that run deeper than this lifetime. By embracing the Christ energy and healing my past, I feel that I am now empowered to move through these issues with no blame attached anywhere.

PETER

My family was Protestant but I was raised with very little emphasis on religion. As I matured, I became lukewarm about Jesus and Christianity. I got very turned off to it and, as a result, I never allowed myself to open my heart to Jesus even though somewhere within me I knew I had a deep, deep love for him. I saw him as an extraordinary Master, but energetically I was closed to him.

When I went back in time, I was a man with a wife and children. I had heard about Jesus and was curious. When he came to my town, I felt such a pull, such a calling to be with him. I was compelled. I wanted to spend every waking moment with him. I left my family because I knew inside that I had to join him and be a part of what he was doing. I was overwhelmed by his presence.

Early in his ministry, the crowds were still relatively small. I became one of his disciples and would perform healings. I was helping many people through his presence and energy; his energy poured right through me. The level of love that I was feeling was powerful.

I was totally devoted to him. His presence in my life brought out the absolute highest in me, just by being around him. That was why it didn't feel like a choice—being with my family or being with him. My heart felt so huge in my embrace of all humanity. When I would do healing, I completely lost all sense of myself. I was swept away in the enormity of who Jesus was.

Then, everything shifted. He told us he was going to die. I felt terribly betrayed. I totally shut down—my heart was broken. I wondered how he could do this to me, or to any of us. I felt that he had the power to completely change the situation, but he didn't do anything about it. He just submitted to what the authorities wanted to do, which was to crucify him.

Without his presence, I wasn't able to maintain the huge expansiveness in myself. I just collapsed and became bitter and resentful. I saw some of his other followers being persecuted for speaking out about him. As I pulled back from everyone and did nothing, my fear and resentment took over.

The rest of my life was extremely difficult. I wandered around aimlessly. I had this gift of healing within me, but I refused to use it. I was too angry, bitter and afraid. My fear of being considered as one of his people was even stronger than my anger. What was once an open heart turned into a very soured, closed and embittered one. I died that way—shut down, confused, feeling betrayed.

I could see the parallels between that life and my current one very easily. In this life now, my talents as a healer are extraordinary, and yet I have done a lot of "start and stop" with regard to coming forward with my abilities. I have felt tremendous fear of persecution.

Through the workshops, however, my energy cleared and became so pure and beautiful. I reawakened my extraordinary connection with Jesus and the powerful love I feel for him. In my healing work since, I have often been astounded at the quality and power of energy that has come through me, and I have always felt that its source was in some other time and place. Now I understand this. It is the Christ Consciousness pouring through me.

I'm still healing aspects of myself that are shut down. I'm still learning to embrace my pain and let my joy come out. It's been a long journey for me and there is still work ahead, but I feel more whole than I ever have. I feel blessed to be reunited with him.

RHONDA

I had a very strong upbringing in the Catholic Church, although I haven't been involved with it for a long time. I couldn't find anyone who radiated the level of light and teaching I needed at my stage of evolvement. However, I still hold the Church in very high esteem. I always felt it supported me well, and I never felt any conflict with it. I still celebrate the holidays and do attend services occasionally. I've always had a close relationship with Jesus through the Church and this still sustains me.

I did this workshop twice. In the first workshop, I relived being a carpenter who made wooden barrels. From the first moment I heard Jesus speak, I left everything to follow him and to share his message with others. I was so excited and filled with the spirit of love and Christ energy, that I could barely contain myself!

I didn't remember much about the trial and the crucifixion. All I remembered was his total acceptance of the work of his Father, and the joy that he had even in his so-called greatest pain. He was transfigured by the event, and I stood in front of him in absolute awe. I was so surprised that I felt no anger or pain about his leaving. All I saw was the joy that comes from doing the Father's will.

During the crucifixion I felt the earth's outrage—the black clouds, the lightning, the earthquakes. There was a shudder. The skies went dark. The decision I made upon his leaving was that now there was nothing left on Earth worth saving. I felt that a great light had gone out here and I decided that I would never come back to this God-forsaken place. I guess I was more angry than I knew.

After the crucifixion when Jesus returned, he told us of the importance of keeping the Light alive. He foretold of the period of darkness ahead and told us that the battle to keep the Light burning was worth the effort. But all I could see was the density of the planet. I had lost hope that the new day would arrive and I was afraid of giving people what I thought was false hope and of leading them to their death. But I put my own fears aside and did as Jesus asked.

I continued serving the light, but there was a deep part of me that was frightened that the light would never survive in this place.

There seemed to be so much struggle involved and not enough support on the Earth for it. But I carried on and lived out my days doing my best to foster Jesus' message.

This workshop gave me deeper insight into many people's conflicts with both organized religion as well as Jesus himself. It opened my eyes to the struggle of others. My perspective has always been that religion has kept the light alive, even though the leaders made some mistakes along the way. In the past, I could somewhat understand one's hostility toward religion, but never toward Jesus. I had not connected the dynamics of pain, of loss and of separation from him with one's anger toward him.

In the second workshop, I saw much more clearly how Jesus walked his path of planting light and living God's will as his own path to *his* freedom. I saw how it was his growth. Yes, he was being of service, but my whole perspective on service changed. I used to think that love was something that you gave until you had no more to give. During the workshop, Jesus kept showing me the strength of his connection with God and the Earth, and that he had to be completely solid before he could receive and then, of course, give. The giving was a result of his being so full of God that it was just a natural overflow. That's the major lesson I'm still working on. It has redefined what love means to me—love comes from a place of wholeness.

I also saw that Jesus did not die for anybody's sins. He did it for his own evolution. He was not sacrificing himself.

As a result of the workshop, I cleared much of my unworthiness issue. Before, I felt I could never give to the extent that he did. My Catholic orientation made me feel as though I could never measure up to him. Now, I know I am on equal ground with him, and it feels like a real blessing to have discovered this. I realize that's the way he's always wanted it. He was just waiting for me to get it!

My misinterpretation of who he was accounts for my "over-giving." Seeing that he came from a place of wholeness has been such an eye-opener!

MARK

My relationship with Jesus was greatly clouded by my Protestant upbringing. I came into the workshop not knowing what to expect; however, I was intrigued so I decided to give it a try.

When I went back in time, I found myself to be a poor man who made things with my hands. I lived in the desert and would sell my wares to the caravans that came through. One day Jesus appeared. I felt such a strong pull of the heart that I couldn't resist, and I left what I was doing to follow him.

My next recollection was being at the crucifixion. I was stung by the indignity and the suffering that I felt Jesus was experiencing. I was heartbroken. It was such a tragic ending. Afterwards, I felt I had lost that part of myself I'd had when I was with him. I was never the same again and became a wanderer.

Many years later, I joined a ship as one of a fighting force of mercenaries. We were engaged in close, sword-to-sword combat with the enemy. I was struck in the chest by a spear and was pitched overboard into the sea. I knew immediately I was going to die, but I didn't care. Ever since Jesus' death about fifteen years earlier, I had been in a haze of numbness. I felt that life was meaningless if such a magnificent one as Jesus could be put to death.

As I drowned, Jesus appeared to me and infused me with his love. I had ceased to believe in the goodness of life, and there, at my last breath, I came to an instant knowing that it was all okay. As I left my physical body, my energy joined with him and I became peaceful again. I felt reunited with my Master and the Christ within me.

Throughout the workshop, I healed much of the pain, loss and separation I had felt in that lifetime. I felt I had realigned myself and restored my heart and openness. My numbness was gone. I felt more awake than I had ever been before.

I no longer see Jesus as a religious figure. I now see him as a pure energy and a pure teacher, devoid of the dogma that is so apparent in modern religion. Experiencing him on a personal level washed away my resentment of the religious approach. What was left was the pure consciousness, the Christ Consciousness.

I also came to appreciate the value of past-life regression. I realized it didn't matter whether it was true or not. And how could I prove it either way? The important point is the emotional opening that had taken place for me.

I had concerns about whether I was actually this man who followed Jesus. I analyzed the improbability that if everyone alive today did this work, there would be no way that they would all have lived in Jesus' lifetime because there simply weren't that many people on the planet back then. What I realized in the workshop was that it doesn't matter. What matters is the healing and connection that takes place as a result of the work. That created a major shift in my perception of it all.

Alison

I was brought up in the reformed Jewish faith. When I was a teenager, I developed a strong curiosity about Jesus. I became so interested in him and the Christian faith that I even considered entering a convent. I remember my mother being quite disturbed by this and sending me to our rabbi to have him talk me out of it. Even though I didn't enter a convent, I continued to be enamored with Jesus. He fascinated me totally. When I was in college, I would argue with my Jewish friends about Jesus and Christianity and, of course, I was always the one on Jesus' side!

In the workshop, I went back and discovered that I was a man who traveled closely with Jesus as one of his inner family. I loved Jesus dearly and whenever he spoke about God and our love within, I was always deeply moved. I felt his purpose alive in me and it seemed to ignite my own need to touch others as he did.

When Jesus was crucified, I was stunned. I heard sounds of anguish escaping from me that were wild and animal-like. I was so grief-stricken that I didn't know what to do. I became a companion and guardian to some of the women, including Mary, who had been closest to Jesus. However, I stopped speaking, and my vision was very blurry as my eyes were always covered with tears. The grief I felt was so overwhelming that I felt I could cry forever. I lived to be an old man and felt this way until the day I died.

Through the workshop, I healed my grief and despair. My feelings of loss had been deeply buried in me and, in feeling them again, I opened the way for my love to really express.

I do love Jesus so very much. Now in my meditations, I experience him as a physical presence—a humorous, sensitive, strong, light-filled presence. I realize that my feelings for him when I was younger stemmed from my strong past connection with him. I knew him well in that lifetime and I'm truly glad to be so close to him again now.

MICHAEL

I didn't remember much about the details of my lifetime with Jesus, except that I was one of his disciples. But I do remember the energy I felt very vividly. It was astounding. I was talking in the workshop about how I couldn't remember much, when suddenly a powerful wave of light started to come through me. I knew it was the Christ energy. It was electric and it seemed to affect every group member very strongly. It reverberated right through me and touched everyone in the room. My wife, who was standing next to me, started sobbing; for years she had not been able to emote this way.

Another member of the group also started sobbing and I embraced her. Soon the whole group was being moved by this Christ energy. It was beyond what my mind or anyone else's mind could comprehend. I remember Deborah commenting that she had never witnessed such energy coming through in all the workshops she and Jack had done.

I refer to it as the most powerful and truly beautiful experience I've ever had. As a result, my heart opened and I had a direct relationship with Jesus. I had been brought up as a Congregationalist and then became an agnostic. Along the way, I had become very turned off to Christianity and turned toward the Eastern and native spiritual traditions which I found much more meaningful and inspiring.

I now feel a strong connection with the Christ energy, and I see the power of it in each of us. I see Jesus as one of the many Masters. This experience fueled my desire to have and to live the reality of the Christ Consciousness all of the time.

ALEX

Raised Presbyterian as a child, I soon rebelled against my religion because it felt empty. I never held much regard for religion and I still don't. For me, the dogma of religion has prevented the true teachings of spirit from coming through.

Before the intensive, my relationship with Jesus was negligible. I considered him "the Son of God" in the sense that we all are.

When I went back on my journey, I found myself to be a thief who stole for my livelihood. I had learned my "trade" early on as a boy living alone in the streets. Although I had many close encounters with the law, I always managed to escape punishment. Clever and cunning though I was, I did eventually get caught stealing and the punishment was crucifixion.

I suddenly found myself stumbling to my execution site with a cross on my back. I saw two other men about to be crucified as well. One was Jesus of whom I had never heard.

I was aware of my anxiety and fear of dying. Once hoisted up on the cross, I glanced at Jesus who was next to me. Our eyes made contact and suddenly a great peace enveloped me—I felt unafraid. I was awestruck by his loving presence, his caring and obvious gentleness. Although I couldn't hear words, I felt him sending me a message of peace and acceptance. I could see he felt this way about everything that was happening to him.

Soon I left my body and after my death, I was aware of his presence again. His energy was moving, comforting and transporting. I was able to see that lifetime in a completely different light. I realized, because of Jesus' love, I had been transformed. Suddenly, I understood the concepts of everlasting life, love and acceptance. It was beyond forgiveness. Forgiveness was not even an issue. It was a simple allowing of who I am. I saw I now had choices and could live my next incarnation differently. I felt freed and empowered.

In my current life, I have always been such a "law-abiding citizen." It was interesting to see myself as a common thief with no conscience. It gave me an understanding of what it feels like to be unconscious and not know anything different. My moment of "waking up" in that journey was so brief and yet so profound. Realizing I had choices changed everything. All of this came out of one brief, powerful exchange with Jesus.

Now my relationship with him is a very personal and meaningful one. I know he is a Master and a beloved friend who is here for all of us. His presence is comforting and he is completely available. Whenever I feel disconnected from him, I know it's me, not him. Then it's quite easy for me to reconnect and feel one with him and the Christ energy.

If any of these stories has disturbed or upset you, let this be. Don't judge the stories or yourself. Instead, understand that your perceptions are being rearranged and this is in accordance with your own highest well-being. You are being realigned to fit your true nature. We encourage you to trust the thread of the energy you feel so it can show you what is on the other side of your disturbance—love.

Because time has no meaning in the context of the soul, a pattern established two thousand years ago could be in place just as firmly this very day. In fact, the pattern may be in you even more firmly because it has no doubt been reinforced by experiences in other lifetimes. The ruts are worn deep and we may find ourselves stuck. Obviously, we want to strengthen the qualities that promote growth and transform those that limit it. We feel this is the key to restoring ourselves to the wealth of love that Jesus showed us was already possible within us.

In reading this material, you may have found yourself identifying patterns within you that were seeded in your time with Jesus. Certainly a number of obvious ones are worth highlighting—true and deep unconditional love, following an inner calling, knowing union with God, healing and performing miracles through God's

power, co-creating, forgiveness and compassion. All are patterns
that were firmly reinforced, if not learned anew, by being with Jesus.
Other patterns that might have been seeded then, and which we
will address in greater depth, include deciding that it's dangerous
to express one's light, feeling guilty or unworthy, staying small, or
numbing the pain either by going crazy, giving up, or getting vio-
lently angry.

So much has been written about Jesus' teachings, yet relatively
little is known about him as a person. It was his "personhood" and
his love, reflected through his daily contact with us, that still moves
us the most. It was his own demonstration of living what he taught
that has stayed in our hearts long after his physical passing, and
this inspiration lights up our own Mastery.

One theme we saw appear consistently in all the workshop participants' past lifetimes with Jesus was that none of them had yet
developed their spiritual fiber strongly enough to hold the Christ
energy fully after Jesus' departure. This is one of the biggest les-
sons we have been learning since then—to build and strengthen
our own spiritual fiber.

In some of the stories, you will note that people found themselves playing different roles each time they journeyed back. We
have seen this to be true for ourselves as well. Both of us have
taken this journey many times, and each time we have been a different player. There is purpose and blessing in each experience.

Our years of doing this work have shown us that these "regressions" are simply windows through which our spirit can give us
insight and education directly relevant to our current life *at that
moment*. Each journey restores, clarifies and enhances us even more.

Chapter Six

Through Jesus' Eyes

We have all projected so much of our own fear, horror and judgment upon the way Jesus was treated that we have not stopped to think that perhaps it wasn't this way for him at all. We have made a lot of assumptions about this man. Therefore, we feel it is essential to understand Jesus' lifetime from his point of view.

While still at the cabin, Jesus came to us one day and told us he had a big surprise for us. He took us back in time, yet again, and this time he had us merge with him so we could see, experience and understand his lifetime from his perspective. This was both astounding and very illuminating. It was such a leap from where we had been in terms of our own projections about him and the events of his lifetime.

Prior to this journey, we had begun to understand that he hadn't suffered the way we thought, but we certainly were not yet at a level where we could fathom how it really was for him. Once again, it was time to dissolve our preconceived notions. He encouraged us to stretch ourselves and *be him*. In order to do this, we had to let go of our unworthiness and be willing to be big—very big—in ourselves.

In taking this journey, we reached new heights of understanding and were able to fully appreciate his level of evolvement. This expanded us enormously. When we experienced his deep dedication, we understood clearly why he responded the way he had and why he made the choices he did. Grasping how it was for him broadened our vision to understand the depth of purpose and love of God in ourselves. It is, we feel, an essential experience for us all.

As with your own personal journey back two thousand years, this one can also be repeated many times. Every time we have done it ourselves, it has lightened and strengthened us even more.

The following narrative is a combination of our experiences of this journey with Jesus. At some point you will note that we move from the "we" term to "I." This denotes that we have merged with Jesus and are now experiencing events *as him*.

As you read this story, we encourage you to open your heart and mind so that you can move into him. Let him carry you in *his* heart and mind while you "walk in his shoes." Recognize, of course, this is what we experienced. What you experience could be different.

Jesus instructed us to relax, close our eyes and take some slow, deep breaths. Before we knew it, he lifted us up and took us to a very special meeting place. It was not Earth. It was another dimension, very sacred and protected. The energy here was rarified and light. As we grew accustomed to it, we could make out forms that seemed to be Light Beings gathering around an enormous table in the middle of an exquisitely beautiful room. The air was soft and the vibration tranquil. Everyone seemed to be talking quietly until we came in, at which point the room grew silent. All eyes came our way and settled intently on Jesus. The feeling of honor and privilege was in the air.

Jesus nudged us gently, motioning us to sit down. He went to stand at the head of the table as he was obviously the guest of honor. As we gazed upon him, his energy became golden and very bright. We could feel the intense love vibrating between him and these other Beings. We sensed that they were very much a part of what was to come, even though they wouldn't all be in the body for it. Many of them would be just as instrumental as Jesus, yet they would remain far from the Earth's atmosphere. This was clearly a group undertaking.

Jesus moved his gaze gently over to Mary. What love there was between them! It was palpable. It made us melt inside. He acknowledged with respect that she was to be his mother in this upcoming incarnation. Next, he gazed over at Master St. Germain. They shared a wink and a smile. Jesus acknowledged that St. Germain was to play the role of his father. The three of them joined hands and as they did, the energy among them started to grow bright and strong. We could feel their intensity of purpose becoming focused and direct. They were intent upon one thing: their mission to plant light on planet Earth. Suddenly, they began to vibrate as they prepared themselves to change dimensions. As they were leaving, we all stood and infused them with our love, confidence and support. This was a mission of God, a great and wondrous thing that was about to take place on the beautiful planet Earth. At that moment, Jesus pierced us with his eyes and we suddenly dissolved into him until nothing was left of ourselves. We had become him.

I find myself traveling very quickly toward Earth. I know that Mary and Joseph have been there long before me and are ready to receive me now. Like a flash, I enter Mary's body and am instantly immersed in a great cocoon of warm fluid and gracious contentment. I am here. I am in Mary, as my mother, on Earth. I am still very small and yet I am alive and as sentient as I will be the day I am born.

I spend the months in close union with Mary, she and I bonding and learning from one another in this special way. I love her deeply. I love my father, Joseph, also. The bond I have with my parents is strong and mighty. It is the bond not only of parent and child, but also of co-patriots in full service to their mission.

When it is time for me to be born, I come easily and swiftly into the world and am struck by how bright it is. Everything shimmers and is so beautiful. Around me I see many faces beaming. They love me and are welcoming me into this place. I feel good here, very good.

I grow up as a boy with a great deal of love, laughter and support all around me. Not only do my parents care for me, but also my friends' parents as well. We are one big happy family and the love flows abundantly. We are simple, generous people. I know I am different. I see the "unseen" as well as the "seen." I am always in the presence of my angelic friends.

When I walk out in nature, I see the trees and the animals, and I also see the fairies, devas and elves. Magical energies envelope me everywhere I go and I am touched by all of them. I love to talk to them and commune with them.

Gradually, I start to recognize that not everyone is as happy as I am. In a way, this surprises me and yet it doesn't. I am curious about people and in my exploration of them, I see that many live desperate lives filled with struggle. They seem afraid. I look into their eyes and witness their lack of connection with God, with all of life. They all have good "reason" to feel the way they do, but I know that this "reason" is false. I see that God is all that matters.

I love spending time with my father in his workshop. He has many projects and he lets me help him. He is teaching me about working with wood and the skill and patience this requires. He also speaks to me of responsibility and of being true to myself. He is a gentle, compassionate man and I find his presence strengthening and soothing.

As I grow, I am schooled in religion like the rest of my friends. I develop quite a rapport with my teachers because I am a good and eager student, but soon I see that my questions are disturbing to them. They just want me to be quiet and that is not like me; I am too inquisitive. They want me to simply accept what they are teaching me as law. As I get older, the gap widens between my so-called "teachers" and myself. My parents tell me it is time to go away and learn from others what I cannot learn here. Although I don't want to leave my family and friends, I am excited at the prospect.

I go far away to an area that is now known as India. I study with many Masters and sages who teach me many things. I learn how to master my own energy. I learn how to discipline my mind and my body, how to reach freedom far beyond thought. I am opened to other dimensions of consciousness, and I am trained in interdimensional travel and communication. I study everything that I will be needing later. I am aware now that I am on Earth with a mission. I know I need to strengthen myself deeply in order to carry it out.

I practice out-of-body, etheric traveling during these years away. I go to different parts of the world and establish connections with the places and people who will be a part of my planting of light. I am building a massive energy network. It is a good time for me, a time of intense discipline, learning and the witnessing of my profound abilities. It is not always easy, but it is always enormously rewarding.

Finally, I am ready to return to my homeland. I know the work that I am to do, but I realize that there is one last preparation I must make before beginning my ministry. I go deep into the desert to cleanse and purify myself. During this time I surrender my will to God, to my Father. I cleanse and purify my heart so that my heart is no longer my heart, but His heart. I give up my mind, my thoughts of myself and any worldly desires. I dissolve into Him and we become one. At the end of my forty-day sojourn, all of my will is gone; it is now His will and His alone. He tells me I am ready and that now it is time for me to go forth among the people. I go forward, light-filled and purposeful.

I begin my ministry simply by talking with those who will hear me. I speak to them about the love in their hearts, about their goodness and about God within them. I tell them that they do not need to live in despair and darkness because they are shining inside. At first, there are but a few who hear me, but quickly those few turn into many. Soon we are a family of wanderers moving from town to town, lighting the way for others. Those moments that I have with each person with whom I come in contact are precious. When I touch their hearts, I know I am igniting the candle within them so that their light is bright and clear. I can see their love for me is creating change in them.

Many do not know what to do with these new feelings, but that doesn't matter because I know they will find their answers eventually. Everywhere I go now, there are more and more people. It seems as though they cannot get enough of me, enough of hearing about their own goodness. What a wondrous thing it is!

Many who come to me are deathly ill and I am able to heal them. They perceive my healing as a miracle, and I see that they don't understand that I am simply acting on the perfection that they already have within them. It is important that I demonstrate this perfection to them. I am teaching about the power of God. The more healings I do and the greater "miracles" I perform, the more people see that God's power is undeniable.

I have many who are part of my "family." When I look into their eyes, I see the love and devotion they have for me. I know that ultimately they will need to find the love within themselves, for themselves. I know the time will come when they will need to have their own direct connection with God without me being their messenger. But the time is not yet, and I see they are not yet ready.

I love them so. I love all of these people, those that are close to me and those that have not yet come. I am constantly filled with God's light and there seems to be no end to this consummate abundance. I cannot help but reach out; the joy I feel in doing so runs very deep in me. I am grateful for this time of sharing. I am all the wiser and better for it as well.

During this time, I stay close with my mother, Mary. Although we are not physically together very often, we are very much in communication vibrationally. One night, she comes to me in my dreams and tells me that things will be changing soon. I feel myself hesitate for a moment but it soon passes. She tells me to remember her strength and take it as my own when I need it. I love her. I am grateful.

My days and nights continue to be filled with joy, harmony, peace, laughter, sharing, teaching and loving. There is endless activity around me, and I am thankful for those dear ones who take such good care of me. I know that my message is growing stronger. I know that I am becoming a "force of Light to be reckoned with."

When several of my disciples come to tell me of the dissension that is developing around me, I am not surprised. I am not worried and I tell them so. I know I AM God's will and all is going *completely* according to His plan. I continue to go about my way of speaking out and opening hearts. I know I am creating waves— earthquakes, one might say. I am strong and resolute in my purpose and I continue on with it.

The crowds continue to get larger and larger. I know both the government officials and the religious leaders are threatened by the bond of trust that I am developing with the common people. These common people are my kind, and they are the ones who can receive my message. They are finding a sense of independence that they didn't know they had. This obviously is not appreciated by those in power, those who want to maintain control.

I know that soon everything is going to erupt. I gather those who are particularly close to me and tell them what is to happen. Most of them cannot hear my words. They do not believe that I would really let this happen. They know I am capable of miracles, so they convince themselves that I will put a stop to it all. They put on blinders and wait for me to change things. I will not. It is not my Father's plan.

Soon I am tried and found guilty. I am going to be killed, to be crucified.

I feel the presence of my mother's strength and reassurance with me. I feel an urgency to surrender more deeply into my Father's heart. I know what is coming is going to be very powerful, and I want to be ready. I pray. I pray for myself and for these blessed people. I pray that they will see themselves and their radiance clearly. I pray that they will understand and have compassion for one another. I pray that they will not forget their light.

I feel the weight of the cross heavy on my back. I am a strong man, but this weight tests me well. I have had communications with some of the soldiers who are feeling remorse for their role. I know I cannot do their forgiving for them, but I have done my best to show them that they are helping me, not hurting me. In their eyes, I see this is still too large a concept for them to understand, but I know there is divine orchestration about all that is taking place. Someday they will, too.

I look around and see the eyes of many people. I hear screams and cries of anguish, voices of rage and rebellion. It's as if I am seeing it all through a mist of light. All the noise seems to be on the outside, while inside all I can feel is love, love for myself and love for God, love for these people and love for this beautiful Earth. I know where I am going. I see that they do not—yet.

I am hoisted up onto the cross. My hands and feet are wounded with nails; I am bleeding. I feel distant from my body, and I see it as though I am outside of it now. My training in India prepared me for this and I am easily able to transcend the pain. I look down at the people, and I see that they misunderstand what is happening here. I wish they could all see into my heart. I know that they are all screaming for my pain—pain which I do not have. They are crying for my suffering—suffering which I do not know. They think they are crying for me, but they are really weeping deeply for themselves. They think their hearts are breaking because I am leaving them. In truth, their hearts are breaking because they are abandoning themselves. I am not leaving them and I will soon show them this. They don't understand any of this, but someday they will. I open my eyes to them one last time, and my heart speaks this message, "It is not as it appears to be. Look within to know the truth. Love and forgive."

I see light blazing everywhere and I feel the presence of many hosts of angels. There are many Beings calling to me. I feel my Father in my heart. My body is dying but I am not. My heart stops beating but my spirit does not. I look around and feel a sweeping joy for what I have done here. I have succeeded in my purpose; I have fulfilled my mission. Everywhere I look, I see the light planting itself into the Earth, into the ethers of all consciousness there. It is pouring in, abundant and glorious. I know that this place and these people will never be the same. They have been ignited. God has triumphed! What a glorious thing this is. I am fulfilled.

I slowly ease myself away from the grieving crowds. I touch them all as I gently pass into formlessness where I stay for a while not thinking, not knowing, just being. When I awaken in my next dimension of consciousness, I see and feel my friends here, the many Masters that I had met before I came. They are celebrating and inviting me to join with them. They are most pleased and so am I. We are proud. It is a moment of great exultation for all of life everywhere!

I gaze down upon Earth, and I see a ring of bright fire circling her. I see a similar ring inside the hearts of those that I touched. I know this ring of fire will spread itself and, over time, everyone will awaken to this sweet flame within them. I get myself ready to return to Earth and show them that I have lived on regardless of my physical death. It is yet another demonstration that God lives eternally. Deep within them, they will recognize this sign and gradually they will teach themselves to live by this truth in dignity and freedom for all. Hallelujah!

Chapter Seven

Project Lightstar:
Birthing the Christ Consciousness

Soon into our time at Lighthouse we were presented with an opportunity to develop an internship for four special people. They had each requested that we offer more advanced training than we had done to date. Upon examining this possibility with the Masters, we were instructed to conduct a ten-week program that was to be called Project Lightstar.

Initially we thought it was simply an internship for the four, but very soon into our time together, we found out differently. We were told the purpose of the project was to birth the Christ Consciousness. The work we were doing at Lighthouse was dismantling the old Jesus paradigm thus making way for a new paradigm more befitting modern times. It was making way for the matrix of the Christ Heart—pure, sacred and inviting.

At the time, this information seemed much too big for the two of us to fully grasp. Although we understood partly what was going on then, we have only recently, years later, gained clarity about this project as a whole, as the global project that it was.

While writing this book, Deborah, in meditation with Jesus, asked whether or not we should devote a chapter to Project Lightstar. Prior to this, we had felt it was simply our own sacred experience tucked away with our sacred memories. Apparently Jesus had other plans. When asked if he would define both the project and the purpose of sharing this information, he responded as follows:

"Project Lightstar was designed to bring the etheric energy of the Christ Consciousness paradigm into a more solid physical reality than ever before. The actual substance of the etheric patterning was being poured through you as you opened your arms and cells as a conduit for this light energy. You felt as though you were an empty vessel that had been deliberately prepared for service in this way. You were empty, available and able to hold your center together whilst a very large amount of Christ light poured through you and was anchored through Jack into the waiting cells, both of the Earth herself and into the etheric band of human consciousness.

"In your mind, visualize it like a very large tree that is taking deeper root, spreading itself out further and further to find the nourishment it needs to continue growing. And in so doing, it becomes stronger and more stable, larger and more dense. It reaches more of life as it covers greater mass. This is what an "etheric planting" of this nature does. The energy is gradually brought through the different dimensions of form, each one more dense than the one prior. With each level of form, it gains in substance—it is literally like an idea, a possibility, taking shape into reality.

"Once the idea is substantially formed in the etheric realm, conceivable to human awareness, it can then be 'plucked' by the human consciousness just like ripe fruit from a tree and given three-dimensional life through each individual's experience. The integration part of the equation is entirely dependant upon the free will of the individual and, as you have seen, requires effort and perseverance. This integration is not automatic at this point in time on your planet. Some day, it may be, as more and more of you pull this energy into your living, breathing, daily reality.

"Many have repeated what Jesus did in various times and places, many who have embodied the Christ Light in human form. But at the point of the Lightstar Project, this consciousness (which had so successfully been brought forward through and by others in the past) was now entering a new stage of physical possibility. It was no longer just for the few, but for everyone. *Now, it was coming forth for all to experience—every life form on planet Earth and every human being walking upon her.*

"You might say this is a very radical statement. But the time is now—and you, plus many others who are now reading this book, have known this for quite a while. It is true that you at Lighthouse were not, and will not be, the *only* points of seeding into this deeper realm of physical reality; but, at that time, each one of you came together in complete devotion and service to this purpose and made yourselves available for us to use in this way. This was your love, your passion and your grace. So use you we did—thoroughly.

"The six of you united like a star. You, Deborah, were at the top apex acting as a funnel for the energy to come in. Jack was the bottom point anchoring it into the Earth. Together you held this vibration so that the four interns, who acted as the 'pillars,' could ground it in through the ethers and spill it forth like rays of the sun. All together, you created a symbol of sacred geometry through which this could happen. You were the human elements of the equation which could enable this to be brought forth into the human arena. You gave up everything to do this—each of you—for that period of time.

"It worked! Now this possibility, this idea, is strong enough and substantial enough within the level of consciousness of humanity that it is easily available for anyone who reaches for it. Once the desire to expand in this way is opened in the heart, the Christ crystal lying dormant inside each person is instantly activated. The ease of this now is due, in part, to the work you all did through the project years ago.

"Mount Shasta was the perfect place because of its interdimensional nature. It was the perfect time. The energies were in perfect balance. And there were the six of you to complete the human element of the grid that would enable this to be stabilized properly. This was your mission. This you have done.

"As we said, you were not the only ones involved in this seeding during this time. There were many on your planet who were assisting in this, many without even being conscious of doing so. In sharing this material with the world, you will awaken the knowing within many of your readers that they, too, have been, and continue to be, directly instrumental in bringing this consciousness more fully and more fluidly into the arena of humankind. Awakening to this in themselves will urge them to reach more deeply within to open their own Christ Heart, thus adding greater and greater fuel to the fire of this reality spreading across the globe. It will impress upon them more firmly that the etheric template for this reality has now been established so close into human awareness that it is but a thought and a desire away. It is right here *NOW* for the taking.

"In sharing your Lightstar experience openly with others, it will start them thinking about some of the steps that are traveled as one transitions from the old world into the new world of the Christ Heart. Ultimately, it is not only about the personal journey, but about the lighting of the Earth Star—the goal toward which this very project was working. This information is both important and relevant to all."

With this information in hand, we can now look back on our Lightstar experience with even greater love and appreciation than previously. As we said earlier, even though we were able to grasp parts of what it was about, we were simply unable to absorb the whole thing.

Deborah recalls it clearly, "Although occasionally during the project, we would discuss what this 'birthing' meant to each of us, we never seemed to get very far with it. Somehow the details of it were out of our reach, and I'm sure this was exactly how Jesus wanted it. Oftentimes, less information is best so that we don't get in the way of what is wanting and needing to happen.

"I know I felt the intensity of the whole thing far more than the others because I was closer to it. I knew very well what my role in it was without having to know anything more about it. My role was to stay centered and focused on allowing the energy to pour through me and to surrender to it fully. I loved that part of it the most. It gave me such a deep feeling of inner satisfaction to be so consumed by an energy that was so much greater than myself, as though *all* of me was being thoroughly expressed and used. It was a powerful, purposeful experience and one which I could feel was stretching me beyond my previous scope of ability.

"The hard part about it for me was that, at times, I felt so open and so 'electrified' with energy that I thought I couldn't stand it. I felt like one giant nerve ending that was raw and over-stimulated. At these times, the smallest things felt irritating whether it was too much human activity around me or even just the wind blowing! It was challenging for me to find ways to soothe myself when I felt this way, and I remember a number of times going into the walk-in closet off of our master bedroom, closing the door and just sitting in the dark amongst the clothes. What a relief! I felt like I was in an insulated cocoon that blocked out at least the outside stimulation and enabled me to feel quiet inside. I'm sure I'm not the first person who has ever found peace in a clothes closet!

"Toward the beginning of the program, I was shown more of what the project was about. While meditating, I felt myself 'slipping out of my skin' in very slow motion. At the same time, I was aware that I was moving somewhere very fast yet, when I looked around me with my inner vision, nothing looked any different than it had a moment ago. 'That was weird,' I thought to myself, 'I could have sworn I was just traveling somewhere.' No sooner had I thought this then I realized that, 'No, in fact, something *is* very different here.' I was gazing at what I thought was Earth, yet the feeling of it, the sensation of the energy was remarkably different from any-thing I had ever felt on Earth. It was as though everything was lit up, love-filled, singing, shining, shimmering. I thought to myself, 'This must be a twin planet to Earth.'

"I was being shown another planet that was an exact replica of Earth in every way physically, but was spiritually far ahead of us. It was expanded, we were dense. It was evolved, we were not. It occurred to me that perhaps this was what we would become at some point in our great, distant future. I decided I would focus on the energy of that 'twin Earth' and in doing so, I might be able to merge it into my identity of Earth as I knew it today. With this thought, I returned to where I was sitting at Lighthouse and heard Jesus say to me:

" 'I am showing you what you could call the *overlay world*— the etheric template of Christ Consciousness that is gradually merg-ing into the existing matrix of human consciousness. Over time, and with increased acceptance, this will assume a natural position as the governing vibration on Earth. The two worlds will have merged as one.'

"I found this intriguing because it was exactly what I had sensed. I knew in my heart this was a reality that could truly be manifested. At this point, Jesus said to me:

" 'Take your energy off this for now, and focus yourself on the daily events at Lighthouse. The broader purpose will take care of itself. All you need to do is focus on loving, being loved and shar-ing the wealth of this with whomever comes here.' "

Meantime, back at Lighthouse, we were very busy with people coming from all over the country to take our workshops and do private work and retreats with us. Amongst all of that, of course, was the Lightstar Project—working with the interns and living together with them in our spiritual family cocoon. It was a time of intense spiritual activity, deep love, great magic and enormous unfolding for us all. Throughout our time together, we were to learn the difference between living in the three-dimensional Earth world as we had known it, versus living the Christ Heart in the overlay world that we were now discovering. Through the project, the six of us would literally shift from the old matrix to the new one. What we did with that experience once the Lighthouse phase of the project was over would be entirely up to us.

At the beginning of the project, the two of us vividly remember walking down to the stream to see where each of our four interns—Water, Lion, Rose and Sky—had staked their "tent homes" for the coming two and a half months. Each of them had been instructed to find a place outside on our twenty acres to live during the course of the program. This is where they would sleep and have their own private spaces, while all other needs of daily living would be met in the retreat house among all of us as a group. Having them sleep outdoors would keep them close to nature, allowing her to play an active and directing role in their spiritual awakening.

As we meandered down to the stream that first evening, we gazed at their new "homes" nestled peacefully throughout the woods. It had the look and feel of a small Native American village. For both of us it was *déjà vu*—we had been in this scene often in other times, other places. We could almost hear the hustle-bustle of ancient tribal activity drifting through the trees, the sound of moccasins padding softly on the earth to the beat of a distant drum. It was heart-warming with a strong sense of community and purpose. New birth and awakening most definitely were in the air.

The Masters had told us the entire ten-week period of the project was to be considered a "spiritual journey" on all levels. Each student was to have at least one private session with us per week as well as attend our weekly group session. The four interns were also required to attend all the workshops held at Lighthouse during the period of the project, in addition to attending two other workshops designed specifically for them. It was going to be a time of intense activity for all.

Early on, the daily routine for the six of us began to take shape. Sky, a skilled yoga teacher, led us in yoga early every morning, getting us loose and centered for the day ahead. During the rest of the daytime hours, except when they were busy in session with us, the four interns were free to follow their own rhythms—meditating, resting, reflecting, doing their inner work, hiking, swimming or just hanging around with each other. They were also in charge of all the house cleaning and food shopping for Lighthouse as this was part of their dharma, or joyous daily service.

The two of us had our hands full with the day-to-day demands of Lighthouse—working with other clients, running the retreat center as well as attending to the interns when needed. As often as we could, the six of us would get together in the late afternoons and go swimming in the beautiful alpine lakes of Shasta. We were in God's country and we took full advantage of the bounty there.

The evenings were some of our most precious times together. We would often join in a "group cooking extravaganza," sitting down over our scrumptious, wholesome meals with lots of talk about how we were each doing and what we were learning about ourselves and life. Sometimes these evenings included tears and memories of old shadows, but more often they were times of laughter and stories that we would treasure forever. As different as we were from one another, we were each love-centered Beings devoted to God. Our determination to know the highest in ourselves and each other united us as one. This, coupled with the greater presence and purpose of the project, enabled us to merge as one true "spiritual family."

Soon into our time together, we realized this experience felt remarkably familiar and recognized we were actually reliving our Jesus family experience of two thousand years ago. It was as though the past had come directly into our present and was lifting us to new heights of loving awareness. We felt Jesus strongly with us as he enveloped us in a cocoon of love that he fondly referred to as the "cradle." He explained:

> "We are together with you as a family. It is a family of multitudes because there are many, many Beings involved with this project

on many different levels. The 'cradle of love' that you are in here is all of our love united. We call it the 'cradle' because it is the symbol of nurturing and receptivity. We are not implying that you are in a 'baby stage.' Rather we are referring to the safety and the perfect conditions of love and support that are here for you as you mature, fulfill your purpose and embrace your Mastery. It is the symbol of your own love, your own Christ Heart, emerging within yourselves."

Being in this "cradle of love" touched each of us profoundly. In the face of it, we couldn't help but surrender to its love. It moved us gracefully out of the narrow, tight structure of our somewhat "sophisticated and worldly" selves into the expanded, overlay, love-centered world of the Christ Heart. The two of us watched compassionately as the four interns were effortlessly "stripped" of their layers of defensiveness and hardness, the outer armor behind which they had hidden for their own "survival." This had already happened to us at the cabin and we knew just how it felt.

As these layers crumbled within each of the four, what typically followed were feelings of being startled and uncomfortable, vulnerable and exposed. It was disorienting and unfamiliar to them. And yet, as their true purity and innocence were revealed, they were exhilarated to experience their newfound freedom and freshness of spirit.

Each layer that dissolved was like a death of self into a rebirth of Self. We each knew this experience of "dying to the old" would happen many times throughout our journeys of awakening, like the onion shedding a layer with each rotation toward the center. And each time, it was only through our acceptance and allowance of this release that our authentic natures would have the space and freedom to fully emerge.

The interns had to learn more than ever before, as we had, that their state of "innocence and vulnerability" was not the weakness that the mass consciousness typically perceives it to be, but a blessing which would reveal the true strength and grace of their spirit. In their nakedness, they could feel God touching them—and they could touch back.

As Rose stated so well, "I had always been a 'care-taker' of others, never considering myself worthy of spending enough time and attention just on me. It scared me because I wasn't sure what I would find if I actually did so—especially for two and a half months! Giving this to myself was my first act of self-love.

"As the project got underway, I felt the presence of Jesus so strongly all around me. I had always been a 'closet' Jesus lover and being in his energy, I felt like I had literally 'come home.' I started to relax and automatically felt myself sinking into the comfort of the cradle. Immediately I felt myself being stripped of my old roles and identities, just like old layers of skin peeling away. I thought about snakes and how they shed their skin and realized I was doing the same. It was so quick and effortless that it alarmed me and pulled me up short. My mind moved into a tizzy as I began asking questions such as, 'If I'm not a mother, then who am I? If I'm not a therapist, who am I?' I realized I was afraid to find out, but I was more curious to know. Through this stripping away, I became humble and empty, ready to truly receive myself. I found I was able to accept myself as just a simple Being without any adornment or title by which to define myself. I discovered how incredibly pure and innocent I was, and it moved me like nothing ever had before."

Earlier we mentioned that we had become a spiritual family. The level of support we experienced with each other was so vitally important. We all know the importance and the value of true friendship—the support and feeding that we receive from it, the give-and-take as equal partners. This is what our spiritual family experience was like, only it also included our multi-dimensional families as well—each of our own spiritual guides, friends and angels, including Jesus and the other Masters, as well as the nature energies and intelligences.

We soon found ourselves becoming extremely telepathic and sensitized to each others' needs and states of being. It was as if we were gliding as one body with each of us as individual parts, deeply attuned to, and in harmony with, the whole. It was extraordinary. As Sky states so clearly, "Day by day, I found myself becoming increasingly intuitive and more sensitive to energy than ever before. I knew exactly what was going on with the rest of the Lightstar family most of the time.

"When I looked at why this was happening, I saw that it started when I had let go of my preconceived identities and notions about myself. Suddenly there was all this room within myself—and I opened up. I felt the usual boundaries between myself and other people, as well as between dimensions, diminishing rapidly. It was literally 'blowing my mind' and my 'conditioned circuitry'—my rigidity and previous need to control. I found it very exciting to feel this fluid and interconnected. It was like being given a great present that I could slowly unwrap and savor thoroughly. It was all mine to enjoy and learn about."

As the project progressed, the two of us were amazed at how completely the six of us were melting into a heart, unified whole—the Christ Heart reality. We asked ourselves, "How is it that we could be having such an experience as blessed as this?"

Jack recalls, "It was a rare experience and one that we knew needed to be treated with tenderness and respect. It was like a jewel gracing us with her beauty—and we responded to her exquisite energy by yielding to her, letting her transform us into the beauty we were always meant to be. We realized that this was not some kind of fantastic dream but that, in the sustained presence of true Christ Heart energy, this is indeed what happens.

"As Jesus told me one day:

" 'All of it may seem too good to be true sometimes but what you must understand clearly is that when you live in a reality that is so love-governed, this is what happens. Love heals all wounds and spreads its goodness through you like a vast ocean caressing the earth. Let this knowing motivate you to deepen even more into yourself and embrace your love of your small community here. Set a new standard of living for your future. It can be the paradigm for all to come.' "

We knew this was all happening as a result of our ever-deepening level of commitment to God and to being of service. It was opening us up to new and greater worlds far beyond what we, ourselves, would have even imagined. We reflected on our last few months in Mount Shasta; first we had the cabin experience with Jesus and the Masters, then opening Lighthouse and starting our Ascended Master intensives, and now Project Lightstar.

With each step we took, our devotion and dedication to being "God's instruments" deepened, along with our trust and willingness "to let go and let God." With each deepening of our commitment, increasingly magical things were happening in our lives.

This trust and joy in "dancing with God" was something that the six of us also shared and it made us very happy. It was a deep inner joy of lightness and freedom that bubbled up even in the face of our challenges and despairing moments. Sometimes we were so responsible and "masterful" while at other times we just let loose, playing and laughing like silly, rambunctious children at a birthday picnic. We knew our living together in this special way was time-limited, and we never forgot the spirit of celebration about what we were experiencing.

This joy also pervaded the workshop arena and gave the intensity of our work a lift that was sorely needed given its content. Jack recalls, "In the intensives, I would often watch myself be profoundly wise, loving and compassionate one moment and then, in the next moment, suddenly become the 'jokester.' My natural ability to 'lighten the space' when need be, to transform the solemnity and seriousness of it all, truly began to emerge.

"In dealing with the subject of Jesus, I found that many who came to us had a view that one has always to be pious and proper. I quickly changed that! I soon found that one of my roles was to dismantle this tightness, shake it out, loosen it up and let the joy within spring forth. I witnessed my mastery in this area and appreciated it even though it took many people by surprise!

"With the help and total, willing cooperation of the Lightstar group, I joyfully discovered that this business of Jesus was not only sacred but fun as well. There was need and space for all of it."

Our Lightstar family experienced and expressed the full range of emotions during our time together—there was both intense joy and sadness. As the four moved into their higher aspects of self, they were all faced with their limited and confining behavior—

ways in which they held themselves back and kept themselves small. They each realized how hard they had been trying to "fit in" and belong in the day-to-day world and their frustrations about this were quite evident.

Both Water and Sky had their stories to share about this and it was almost heart-breaking to feel the pain of these two bright, shining lights talk about their years of manipulating themselves and stifling their spirits in order to "be acceptable." Sadly we could each relate to it in our own way. As we listened, each of us reached to reclaim those parts of us that we had so misunderstood. We realized how lost we had felt.

Sky recalls, "As I stayed open to my love and felt it permeating me from deep within, I saw the tightness of my small self more and more clearly. In the past I had tended to compare myself to others, trying to blend and fit in. What a joke! This had done nothing but cause me pain and leave me stranded in a very mediocre place. It became so clear to me that this was a way I had abandoned myself and that I no longer wanted to do this. I was feeling that my uniqueness was too great to hide, my gifts too wondrous to desecrate."

Water explored his feelings even further one day when Jack took him back to his own "home star planet" during a private session. This enabled him to discover his authentic nature thus helping him to further understand and embrace his "differentness" rather than feel at such odds with it. In this exercise, Jack took him on a journey back to a place other than Earth where Water felt completely "at home," where everyone understood him and spoke "his language." It was a place of true kinship on all levels.

Through this experience, Water began to understand his dilemma better than he ever had. He recalls the feeling of his journey, "It was as if I had been a dolphin, completely in my element in the ocean. Then on my next incarnation, I chose to be a human. I knew it was going to be tremendously challenging because I didn't fully understand how humans related. They were different from my way as a dolphin. Suddenly, in my attempt to learn about being human and trying to fit in, I got lost. I forgot that I was a dolphin. Deep inside I pined for who I truly was, my true nature as a dolphin. And once I became aware of my pining and my need to connect with my dolphin nature, I found myself. I realized I came here as a human not to get lost in being human, but to *bring my dolphin qualities here to the human race*. I realized this is my gift to Earth and humanity."

When Water realized that his ability to flow so easily with life and the natural rhythms were his strengths, and that his purpose was to bring them in more fully so that others could learn from him, he was relieved. He could now feel more comfortable in himself in the face of his "differentness."

Midway through the program, the four interns became actively aware of themselves as multi-dimensional Beings. It was all happening by degrees as their boundaries were dissolving and they were becoming more open and available to an expanded network of connection. By listening to the sensitive side of their nature, they deepened their skills to feel and understand energy, which made more frequent and powerful communications with the other dimensions possible. Even though inter-dimensional interplay was not completely new to any of them, their connections were strengthening rapidly and their clarity increasing. It was becoming more and more *real*.

As mentioned earlier, we each had our own spiritual families— guides, teachers, angels. The two of us were already very active with ours, but the interns were eagerly discovering new interdimensional relationships and avenues of love and wisdom previously untapped. They were each beginning to understand their place in the Human family, the Earth family and the Cosmic family. Each one of them was becoming an active and conscious part in the multidimensional family network which the Christ Heart recognizes and embraces so completely.

Jesus spoke to us about our expansion and how our connection to the family of life was helping us to realize our greater selves. He said:

"In your deepening trust of yourselves and God, you are more acutely aware of your place as an important and valuable cog in the universal wheel. You are feeling nourished by the love of Creation.

"In this energy you can relax, play and create, and at the same time be alert, intuitive, sensitive and in constantly flowing communion and communication with the broader elements of your-selves and the intelligence of all life that resonates with you. This enables you to be impulsed by the more evolved intelligence of some of the nature forces and other dimensions around you. They can literally lift you up to a higher plane within yourselves. Your goal and intent is clearly and solidly God—therefore the highest available that you can receive is here to meet and support you. You are reaching for the highest, therefore you are met by the highest and lifted even higher in yourselves. This is what you call expansion."

Shortly after this, evidence of what Jesus was saying demon-strated itself very clearly. The four interns were truly getting a closer look at how their "teachers" were everywhere. It was simply up to them to open their minds and *let them in*. The following experi-ences shared by the interns illustrate how one can explore and ben-efit from one's inter-dimensional support system.

Throughout the project, Lion had several experiences with small animals—squirrels, chipmunks, deer—coming close to her, lying down in her hair when she was asleep on the ground, generally, as she said, "pestering her." It seemed like they were constantly in her face, trying to get her attention—but she would have none of it. For the longest time, she was closed to them because she didn't understand what was happening, and at times she was frightened. For this reason, living outside in her tent had been a challenging adjustment for her.

Her fear and misunderstanding began to shift after she had an experience with several mountain lions down by the stream. She recalls, "During one of the Ascended Master Intensives, shortly before we started on the second morning, I decided to go down to the stream to be alone and just be with nature for a while. I was thinking about what you had both said the night before about living God's will and adopting the attitude of allowing, embracing and inviting in all that we need to experience from moment to moment. I found that I really wanted to experience this depth of openness and acceptance. I was sitting on a big log that spanned the stream with my legs dangling down almost to the water. I closed my eyes and prayed to Jesus, 'Please help me to be open in both my mind and my heart so that I can experience whatever I need for my higher purpose.'

"I sat for a moment feeling the peace of surrender from my prayer as I listened to the stream babbling gently beneath me. The air was crisp and sweet and I felt really good, really in harmony with myself and everything around me. Then I opened my eyes and as my vision cleared, I saw a mountain lion about twenty feet away coming toward me. At first I was totally mesmerized by the sleek beauty of this powerful creature and in awe of its grace. But then my mind kicked in abruptly as it registered that this was actually a lion. I became instantly afraid and began to panic inside. I tried to stay calm, telling myself, 'You can handle this. Just stay open here.' That was fine for all of one second until I saw *another* lion behind the first one also coming toward me. I felt my panic beginning to rise and it hit the roof when I saw yet *a third* lion on the opposite bank! I was surrounded, penned in and they were coming closer.

"There I was on the log with lions on each side and I didn't know what to do. I was frantic and terrified and my adrenaline was pumping fiercely. I could think of nothing except 'How do I get out of here?' Before I knew what I was doing, I sprinted for the nearest tree by the bank and climbed to the top as fast as my legs could carry me. It didn't occur to me until later that it was like thinking sharks can't swim. Of course, the lions could climb the tree much, much faster than I could! But, at that moment I just knew I felt safer in the tree than on the ground. At least they were still down there and I was above them.

"I stayed up in the tree for a while as the lions just kept an eye on me, not moving. I tried frantically to 'shoo' them away—and, of course, that did nothing. They were probably about ten feet or so away from the tree looking at me as though I had rocks in my head. Finally, they seemed to just get bored and moved on.

"Once I knew they were gone, I climbed down from my perch and raced up the hill from the stream as fast as I could. I saw Deborah coming out of Lighthouse on her way down to look for me, and I fell into a heap beside her on the front steps as my legs gave way beneath me and my body shook relentlessly with fear. I literally watched it pulsing through me as though I had truly been in a life-threatening situation. I told her what had happened and she just stayed with me, letting me catch my breath and find my way back to myself. We sat there for quite a while.

"I asked her why she thought this had happened, and she simply said, 'All I know is that there was great wisdom there for you. That will be for you to find out.'

"Once I calmed down, we rejoined the group and I shared the story of my experience. I knew inside that this had, in fact, been a gift for me, but I couldn't seem to stay in that place of clarity and certainty. My anxiety about it was still too fresh and my conditioning to be afraid was too strong. I do remember someone in the group saying to me, 'I know that kind of herding behavior can be typical of lions, but you can count one thing—if they had wanted you for breakfast, you wouldn't be here now.' I also remember Jack saying, 'You must know that those lions had no intention of hurting you, otherwise they wouldn't have hesitated to do so. Their spirit was calling you—that deep part of you which so identifies with them and their spirit.'

"On reflection, I realized it had opened me to the heart and pulse of life and triggered my memory of how important the animal kingdom is to me. I hadn't understood this as deeply before. Living outside, I realized how the animals were helping to bring me gradually and safely 'down to Earth.' I have always known that animals are my allies. They have always been there for me when people have not. What I didn't understand, however, was how *sacred* my connection with them truly is. That's something that I'm still learning.

"The power of that experience stayed with me very strongly afterwards and, although I had begun to see the gift in it for myself, I still shuddered with fear, however slight, every time I thought about it. The presence of this fear alerted me to the fact that I still hadn't totally opened myself to the message.

"Three days later, I felt ready to sit down and recreate the scene so that I could finish my communication with the lions. I knew in my heart they had opened something in me with which only they could help. Their wisdom is what I want to share with you now.

"As I sat quietly and invited them in, I felt myself merging with them. I was surprised at how easily I just seemed to melt into their essence and become as one of them. I felt the strength of their being in my own body, the power and grace of my motion as my legs walked upon the Earth. I felt proud, strong and vigorously alive.

"When I asked them to speak to me and give me the message that I hadn't been able to fully receive a few days ago, they began to laugh softly. It was like a loud purr rubbing up and down my spine, and I knew that they were not laughing *at* me—but *with* me. In that instant, I became aware of how joyful I was to be one of them. How proud and strong and full of life I knew myself to be. They said:

> " 'We are friends of your spirit. When you opened yourself more fully to God's will, we heard your call. Yes, we were prompted to come to you, to forge a new understanding within you of your deep and passionate connection with us in the animal kingdom. Through this understanding, we knew you would gain great admiration for your own strength, agility and courage to soar in the face of life's seeming challenges. You couldn't fully receive us at that time, but you did purge a great deal of your fear, which has enabled us to be so close here now. We are close in your heart always. There is not a moment when you cannot reach for us and drink from our strength and beauty.

> " 'As you accept that your heart is one with the lion, your remaining walls of fear will come tumbling down. You will see yourself standing proud and tall upon the mountain top, and you will hear your soul speak to you of greatness and freedom unfettered. Your power is vast, your passion is deep. Breathe in your grace and you will move as smoothly through your life as we move through the forest—silently, effortlessly, gracefully. Does not this knowing make you breathe a sigh of relief? Does life need to be so hard? Or can you awaken with a great yawn of satisfaction, trusting that all is well? Reflect on these things and we will speak again when you are ready. There is still more to explore about our love together.'

"Through this exchange, I saw that being afraid of them was really me being afraid of the wildness and beauty in myself. I saw and felt their passion, and I knew that their presence in my life was unleashing the hold I have had on my creativity and urging me to break forth with who I am. I felt, and continue to feel, so grateful to them now for coming to me in a way I could not ignore, and forcing me to meet the wisdom in what I was to learn about myself from their reflection.

"Through my experience with all the animals, especially the lions, I have begun to understand that each of us invites into our lives the forces of wisdom that can teach and support us in our return to our sacred center. We are all one with life, so this makes perfect sense to me. I see that, as we are helped, so we then help others simply by our change in attitude. We emit a more harmonious vibration and that affects all of life. When I think about this, I feel strong and empowered."

Like Lion, Rose also had some difficulty with living outside in nature and soon learned that the nature forces were her ally instead of something to fear. She had always had a strong connection with the angelic realms and the fairy kingdom, and one day while she was sitting in her sacred circle next to her tent, they came to her. She recalls, "I remember feeling the energy of the angels and fairies coming into me as I meditated in my sacred circle. I was struggling to feel my spiritual connection by trying to move up and out of my body—my usual way of meditating. This time nothing happened. It wasn't working. Suddenly I heard the fairies laughing! They said:

" 'You know, the way to heaven is through the Earth. You can't get *there* unless you get *here*!'

"Then they took me on a journey deeper and deeper into myself, through my body and into the Earth, until suddenly we weren't in the Earth anymore—we were in the heavens! I thought to myself, 'This is amazing! I never would have found this if they hadn't shown me the way here!' It radically changed my whole perception and understanding of everything. There was no separation for me now."

She had another experience in her sacred circle while meditating, "At first when I would meditate, I would open my eyes with fear, startled with each twig snapping from some animal—a deer, a squirrel, a rabbit.

"One day, I decided to keep my eyes closed no matter what noise I heard. I stayed focused on my meditation, and at the end of it, opened my eyes to find myself surrounded by six deer! The wave of awe that swept over me was mind-boggling. I felt their message was one of safety, love and protection. When I asked them more specifically for their message to me, they answered:

" 'We are here to give you the gift of your lightness and tranquility. We are peaceful in our own hearts and, in our presence, you can open to the greater peace waiting inside of you. We are glad that you were able to transcend your fear of living down here so that we could join with you and reunite in this way. Our family is stronger and more joyous with you in it. We are grateful.' "

Earlier, we mentioned co-creation. The six of us knew that this birthing of the Christ Consciousness was very much a co-creative act. *It was birthed as a co-creative endeavor because the Christ consciousness is a co-creative reality.* In co-creation, we all play a role and have a say in what happens. *It means that we don't just take, we also give.* It means that we understand that everything we do, know and believe has impact upon and affects all other levels of life. It alerts us to our responsibility as creators, not only in the picture of our personal lives, but in the whole as well. We can no longer be weak nor victim-oriented in the face of this understanding. It demands that we step into our bigger, more masterful shoes. Doing so enables each of us to take our rightful place as an equal and capable player in the family of life, rather than feeling separate and alone.

Sky describes his expansion into his greatness, realizing his oneness with all: "I was in meditation in my tent by the stream, experimenting with letting my energy expand as much as *it* wanted. I felt the golden rays of Jesus' energy enveloping me, warm and inviting, compelling me to let go even more. As I did so, I began to feel an inner peace permeating my body and my mind. I spread my arms out wide, focusing on softening and opening, letting my inner Being expand through me like a giant pool of light.

"I suddenly felt this huge presence of energy hovering above my head, pulsating like an intense beam of light. Before I knew what was happening, it had lowered itself into my heart and literally pinned me to the ground. There I lay with this shaft of beautiful light vibrating into my heart chakra, spreading me out, expanding me like a great ocean of love into what felt like infinity. I don't think I could have moved right then even if I had wanted to—its intensity was so strong in my body.

"As the light coursed through me, all sense of limitation and tightness dissolved. I was instantly expanded into a largeness that connected me with the universe and all of life in it. I felt huge, connected, loved and alive. It soothed me, reassured me and purified me. Through its soft yet powerful iridescent rays, I continued to feel the pure golden emanations of Jesus. I suddenly realized that this was the sacred Christ energy in its purest form touching me profoundly. It was the energy of the Christ Star literally illuminating me.

"It moved me beyond words. I knew to stay open to it, to continue welcoming it and expanding myself to receive it. As I did so, its vibrations seemed to caress every cell of my Being, filling me with vital life force and renewed purpose. I breathed fully into it, embracing the energy, and I became still more deeply *one* with it, and *one* with everything. It was like being in a frequency of another place or planet—a much finer vibration than I have ever felt on Earth. All sense of my 'small self' had completely melted away and I had become this very *large* presence, totally connected through my heart with all forms of life everywhere. I felt in pure union with God. It was very powerful for me. I have never been the same since.

"I don't know how long it lasted, maybe only a few minutes. I lay there breathing slowly and deeply as the energy gradually subsided, and I was left in a state of bliss beyond any I have ever known. I have had many profound mystical and kundalini experiences before, but this was the strongest and most profound. I put it in the category of a 'classic mystical experience.'

"Afterwards, I sat there for probably two hours or so just quietly absorbing it all and letting myself be. I remember going up to Lighthouse later and, before I'd even had a chance to tell anyone, my Lightstar family quickly gathered around me wanting to know what had happened that had caused me to look 'so lit up and radiant.' In describing it as best I could, I, again, felt the waves of that pure clear energy pulsating through me.

" 'What you experienced was the true power and blazing light of the Christ Star,' Deborah said. 'This is what is transforming us and our world.' I knew for certain that it was changing me dramatically—I just didn't know specifically in what ways yet.

"Through this experience, I saw and felt how vast I already was. It was so physically impactful that my mind couldn't argue with it. In letting go and truly embracing my spirit in those moments, the beauty, power and strength of it melted my narrow perceptions. It opened me to an experience of connectedness I will never forget. In a way, I felt like this was just a tease for me. It was giving me a tangible glimpse into what is possible if I am willing to truly stand by myself, riding my spirit as *it* carves out my path of freedom. As always, the message was one of trust. Trust myself. Let go and trust myself. I know if I truly live this, I will experience the highest and purest of life in every way.

"Needless to say, the experience of that day has stayed with me in a very potent way. It was very, very powerful for me, and I draw on the energy of it when needed. The night I shared it with the group at Lighthouse, I realized that a spiritual experience like that is a rare gift. It's not designed for one to stay in it forever. I knew that the key was to integrate it into my daily world. That part was yet to come."

These stories are just a sampling of the healing and illuminating experiences the Lightstar four had as they traveled their own paths of awakening in those two and a half months. For everyone who came to Lighthouse during the period of the project, it often seemed like these four interns were the touchstones. They provided a wealth of love, clarity, compassion and strength for all of us to use.

During the workshops in particular, they shone like bright lights eager to share. Sky's mastery came through—his bigness, his ability to hold the energy; Rose's angelic and magical nature as well as her tremendous clarity and wisdom; Water's allowing and flowing nature—always accepting, supporting and assisting with his wisdom; and Lion's tremendous depth of courage and strength of heart ever apparent. They were not only the four "pillars" for us and the birthing, but they were gifts of support for everyone.

In looking back, our hearts are filled with gratitude for that time. We can see how fully the six of us were living the spiritual family community, but with a major fundamental difference from two thousand years ago; this time, in our group of six people there was no *one* Jesus. We were *all* and *each* Jesus! Instead of *one* person fully embodying spirit, *all* of us were. We were now *living* exactly what Jesus had been teaching us many years ago. By the end of the project, we had shifted the matrix from the old to the new and we were actively living the reality of our Christ Hearts. Here at Lighthouse, it was a brand new world.

Leaving the Cradle

"At the end of the Program you will all have the choice to either accept what has awakened in you as a reality within your daily lives or to reject it. This is always a matter of choice. We are not in control of this, only you are."

— *the Masters at the start of Project Lightstar*

When it was time for us to "wrap up" the project, we had a dinner celebration that was full of tears—both joyous and sad. We all knew that our time together in this way was over. The four interns knew they needed to take what they had experienced and learned back into their worldly lives. The two of us knew we needed to rest and regroup.

We, as facilitators, had no idea how difficult it was going to be for them. We knew there would be some difficulty but we didn't know how great. We were still immersed in our "cocoon" of love and safety, continuing on with our workshops and our life in Shasta.

It turned out that it was a *major* adjustment for each of them. In this idyllic setting at Lighthouse, they had lived in conditions that had fed the depths of their hearts and souls. They had nothing or no one to attend to but themselves. The love in the cradle softened and dissolved many of their defenses whereby they emerged "naked and innocent, pure and open." In this exquisitely shining state, they went back out into the world—and the contrast between the two worlds hit them over the head like a two by four.

They were each stunned in their own way. How were they going to cope? How were they going to make this adjustment and take what they had learned back into their previously established lives? They had each become so refined and now their challenge was to "live their refinement." Reclaiming the old armor or "densing up" in order to make this transition back into a world based primarily on fear and survival was not the answer. It would have been simply a perpetuation of an old habit. They each had expanded so much that to try and squeeze themselves back into a smaller, three-dimensional construct was like trying to squeeze the ocean into a coke bottle. This was impossible.

Unfortunately, none of them had any solutions for this "predicament" because they had never walked this journey before at this level of awareness and expansion. They knew they needed to stay true to themselves and learn as they went along. This was a whole new ball game and there were no reference manuals! Later, we would see clearly that this was illustrating, in a magnified way, how it is for everyone who is seeking to integrate the matrix of the new Christ consciousness into the old, patriarchal paradigm. For the four, this situation was more radical simply because they had experienced the Christ world more fully in a removed, concentrated setting rather than gradually through daily world expansion. But the challenges remain the same for everyone, just at different speeds and extremes.

Each of the interns talks about what their reentry was like. Lion recalls, "When I first left the cradle of Lighthouse, I felt very lost. I was afraid that I would not be able to maintain the center I had grown to know in myself and I worried that I would not be able to find my way out on my own. I was scared and it was difficult, but I also knew I had to do it. It was a challenge for me, a great challenge, and I chose to meet it squarely in the face.

"I called on everything that I had learned in those two and a half months. I reminded myself that if I could face up to the challenge in the wilderness as I did, then I could face up to this challenge of 'living in the world' with my abilities intact. I was forced to get really grounded with myself. I remembered the strength and the grace of the mountain lions and I took the feeling of their energy deep inside of me. I remembered all the animals that I came to so appreciate and love. I called on Jesus and felt the Christ in me that I had ignited during that time. I literally willed myself to be present in my life and to be thankful for all that came my way. I would often say to myself, 'I am the Christ Heart, I can do this.' "

Sky recalls his experience, "When I first left the Shasta cradle, I fell apart at the seams. I was overwhelmed, angry and depressed. I wanted to ignore and forget Lightstar. I was forced to really look at my life and, in doing so, I realized how painful it had always been for me to be here on Earth. I didn't want to be here. I was bitter and resentful. I felt as though I had lost the inner strength that I had gained at Lightstar and I didn't know how to get it back. I didn't know how to integrate such total expansiveness into my daily life. In reentering my 'consensus trance' world, I realized how awake I had been in Shasta and I didn't know how to be so awake here. I didn't know how to merge these two worlds as one. In hindsight, it's obvious to me how these reactions were identical to how I had felt when Jesus had died two thousand years ago.

"My emotional pain has been my biggest teacher because it has brought me to my knees many times, forcing me to surrender. I fought my 'bigness' much of the way because I felt so unsafe and unsure with it in the world—yet, I still triumphed, inch by inch, slowly but surely. I realized that oftentimes I have used my anger to keep my openness at bay—and this is something that I continue to work on. I think I need protection but in my heart I know I don't. When I let my struggle go, all my doors of wonder about myself and my world open up again and I am free."

Rose recalls, "When Project Lightstar was complete and I left there, I absolutely knew *who* I was, I absolutely knew *what* I was, and I absolutely *knew* the truth of the world. All this I had gained there. It felt perfect and I wanted the whole world to feel my joy. But I found that I couldn't hold it. I was stunned! I couldn't sustain all that I had learned about myself at Lighthouse out in the world to which I returned. I was a very soft and sensitive Being in what suddenly felt to me like a cold and harsh place.

"Moving out of the cradle was a shocking experience. It was just like I felt when Jesus died. The feeling was one of being completely on my own. In order to deal with it, instead of taking a deep breath and trusting, I panicked. I did what I had done in Jesus' lifetime and in every lifetime since then: I grabbed onto another human being and said, 'Take care of me!' This time I grabbed onto my boyfriend and the more I grabbed, the crazier I felt, and the further I went away from myself.

"Looking back on it now, six years later, I can see that my shock upon reentering my daily world was a big wake up call. It jolted me into action. It didn't feel comfortable at all, but gradually I felt the bubbling up of my desire and ability to take charge of my life. It was up to me to bring my inner and outer pictures into truer alignment. I needed to make the changes necessary so that my external world would be an accurate reflection of my inner world, the truth of my Being. I needed to activate my trust in myself.

"In the last six years, I have learned steadily how to hold that level of light, service, commitment and purpose right *here* in my world. I see clearly that my spiritual fiber has gotten much stronger. I realize that none of the stuff I see around me or my patterns are real anyway, so I choose to just be quiet, be still and return to what's *real*—my own sacredness. It is my *being*.

"I know I have never experienced this kind of strength before. I know love is not something that I do, but something that I AM. To me, this is what the Christ Heart is all about."

Water recalls, "Right after the project was over, I did not return to where I had been living. I decided to go to Maui and take some time to reflect on all that had happened. Shortly thereafter, a group of us went to Australia for six months of intensive body work study. In Australia, I felt like I was also moving in a spiritual family dynamic of a different form. I felt really good that I was, in fact, building on the process Lightstar had started for me. I watched my fellow Lightstar interns struggle somewhat, and I thought to myself that perhaps I had made the right choice because I wasn't struggling at all.

"Several years later, however, life brought me to a standstill. My daughter's mother died of cancer and now she needed me full time. There was no more traveling around the world and fending only for myself. Suddenly I was a full-time parent caring for my daughter whom I love very much.

"This change in my lifestyle altered everything for me as I re-entered my life at a place similar to that of the other interns after they had left Lightstar. Back in a more traditional three-dimensional reality, I was forced to face many of the issues of adjustment that I had avoided. I felt quite lost and weak in the face of this challenge. My self-esteem shattered and my 'bigness' vanished for a while as I was swept up in a tide of internal chaos and fear. I didn't know how to bring it all together.

"In addition to my own inner resources, the supportive network of friends I had built over the years helped me tremendously during this time. I drew upon their feedback as they told me what they saw. They reflected back to me my strength and solidness, my magic and my determination. I took what they told me seriously because I knew it was true. I knew I had to learn how to truly love and respect myself in this environment that had always caused me to feel insecure and unsure of my footing.

"I am continuing to grow in my journey of realizing that my 'differentness' is my greatest value. And I am seeking ways to express my own talents now and really put myself 'out there.' Sometimes I still feel weak and unsure, but through these experiences I am learning about the strength of who I am."

For the two of us, our time of reentry didn't happen for yet another year. During the course of that year, we had continued to expand and deepen ourselves through our continued work with Jesus and the other Masters. We developed new workshops and brought through increasingly higher energy as time went on. It continued to be a time of intense building, learning and refinement for us and our work.

Fourteen months after the interns had left, we were to make the same transition journey ourselves when we left the cocoon of Lighthouse. We were told by the Masters that our two-year project was over. At the outset, we had been told Lighthouse was a two-year project but we hadn't thought of it that way. In fact, we had forgotten! We were joyously in the moment of what we were doing and were not planning beyond the year we were currently in. Not until the end of our second year did we realize the "project" of the retreat center was complete. We still owned our farm in Central Virginia which we had been trying to sell for the past three years. Having been unsuccessful in doing so, we were often frustrated and we had wondered why the farm remained unsold. We soon found out.

In late October, 1992, we received a phone call from our neighbor who was overseeing our Virginia house for us. She had been showing it to potential buyers during a heavy rainstorm. The man had just asked about any leaking problems with the skylights and suddenly water had started to pour through one of the skylights in the kitchen. Our friend said it was as if there had been no glass in the skylight at all—the rain was flooding in! The interested couple had left very quickly.

Our friend kept an eye on the house for the next few weeks, looking to see if the skylight leak got worse. Not only did it not get worse, it never leaked again! When she told us this story, we knew something was going on at the house that we needed to personally check out. We made plans to go back in early November for a week-long visit to see how it would feel to be there and to also check on this mysterious skylight. While we were there, Jack went up on the roof several times with a hose trying to get the skylight to leak—and, of course, it never did.

When our friend had told us the story, she said, "I think some of your spirit friends were up to their tricks. I'm not sure they want you to sell the house." She was right because the moment we arrived, we felt as though the Earth was flooding us with physical strength and nourishment. We hadn't known we were in such need of this more grounded energy. It literally came up through our feet in a way we had never experienced. It was so tangible—our physical systems couldn't get enough of it.

We had expanded so much in Shasta, at such an accelerated rate, and now we were suddenly feeling our exhaustion and our need to be grounded. We felt the effect of such high-voltage energy having run through our systems. It was obvious we were needing to restore ourselves here in the Blue Ridge mountains of Virginia. We went back to Lighthouse to gather our things and "close up shop."

We were torn about leaving the mountain as she was so much a part of our magical lives. On our last day, we went up to say our farewells. As we were sitting there, we could feel her intensity. We felt as though she was saying to us, "Be proud of all you have accomplished here. It is time to take what you have learned out into the world." Soon thereafter we were hurled right out of our energy cocoon and into the three-dimensional reality of Central Virginia.

What a shock it was on all levels! It wasn't something for which anyone could have prepared us. It was just one of those experiences that can only be understood by going through it. It was a dramatic shift of frequencies, dimensions and realities—and we were stunned for quite some time. We didn't know what to make of it as we now felt like completely different beings reentering an old environment in which we no longer fit the way we had previously. It felt like we had just landed here on planet Earth from another galaxy!

We couldn't function well for quite a while. There was a void and a feeling of, "Now what do we do after such an incredible peak experience?" We realized, through our experiences in Shasta, we had just fulfilled a lifelong dream. What we had accomplished and experienced represented a pinnacle of spiritual living that we had been seeking and striving to attain. We asked ourselves, "What is there for us to do now that we have achieved this?"

Our answer was to first integrate and ground this experience fully into our physical system on all levels. What we didn't know was that this was going to take a number of years to accomplish!

This level of integration was a major adjustment on all levels. It took time, love and much patience. There were many new things to understand and mold from a brand new perspective, and a great deal of shedding to go through in the process. Every aspect of our lives was asking to be redesigned. It was so different from where we had just been. In the midst of it all, we didn't always understand that it was simply a process of realignment.

In hindsight, we understood this was the integration of the new matrix of the Christ Heart into our pre-existing, "old world" reality patterns. This integration had to be done if we were to live our Christ Heart fully. It wasn't always comfortable, mainly because we didn't have the clarity and understanding then that we do now. Many of the stumbling blocks were largely a result of internally fighting what was going on, trying to figure it out and make things work "the way they used to" when we were now two completely different people. We had grown far beyond the level of awareness we had prior to Shasta. In later chapters, we will look at many of the stumbling blocks we encountered.

Our greatest help during this time in our lives came not only from the constant support and encouragement of each other, but from our strong connection with the nature world and our friends and teachers in spirit. As Deborah recalls, "I remember so many times turning to a favorite tree while on a walk and asking for a message that would help me through a difficult time. Or I would feel the presence of one of my guides encouraging me to persevere and stay open."

They were always there, steady and supportive, *as long as we reached for them* and made the connection real. We felt they were watching and waiting to see how we would make our moves and what we were learning in the process. This was *our* journey to make and *our* process to understand. With their help, we persevered and rose to meet our challenges. It was extremely strengthening on all levels.

Many years have passed since the Lighthouse period of our lives. It becomes very obvious, as we look back, that our reaction to reentering the world was identical to what we felt when Jesus died. This time, though, we saw that we were completing something in the physical realm which we had been unable to complete then. This time, instead of "losing it and going crazy" or "getting angry and self-destructive," we had the strength and the ability to fully ground and integrate ourselves into our Christ Heart. In this way, we did not need Jesus to do it for us nor to be the support upon which we would lean. All we needed was *ourselves*—full, present, complete and willing. We received ourselves with gratitude.

These last number of years have been a time of deep reward for us as we have grown to fully appreciate the strength of our spiritual fiber. It seems that no matter what happens in our lives, we carry this hum of faith and contentment within ourselves that is unshakeable. From this we continue to grow and expand in true joy.

THE COMPLETION OF PROJECT LIGHTSTAR

Project Lightstar was deeply meaningful for all of us. Experiencing the love, connection and harmony which arose out of our coming together was an extraordinary gift of life. Having it was blissful—leaving it was the hard part. What a metaphor for how it was in our time with Jesus two thousand years ago. We had something so beautiful and sacred, and then suddenly it was over. How were we going to adapt, how were we going to adjust to that kind of sudden shift in energy, frequency and experience?

Two thousand years ago, the six of us didn't handle this shift very gracefully. At that time, each one of us collapsed in his or her various ways rather than rising to meet the shift and move with it in faith and conviction. Now the situation was different. Each one of us chose to face the adjustment and follow through on it. We met the challenges and were strengthened by them—and we continue to be.

It has taken six years for each of us to integrate ourselves and the energy that we seeded during that two and half month period. It was not until a few months ago, while in the middle of this chapter, that we were unexpectedly guided to have a Lightstar Reunion. The ease with which we came together, considering that we were all living in different parts of the country, was telling. It was obvious that this reunion had a special meaning to it and that the timing was perfect.

As we came together, it was soon obvious that the "cradle" of energy we had shared at Lighthouse was enfolding us again as though we had never left it! We spent a glorious week together, reminiscing about our time as a sacred family and discussing openly what had happened for each of us since. Rose voiced it so well, "All the work that we did with you and Jesus and the other Masters during the Project allowed us to fully move into the present. I know that the last six years of my life have been about finishing that move. It has been about my allowing the last little residues of anything that would hold, confine or limit me to a certain belief system or concept of self to be washed away.

"To me, that's how Lightstar has translated itself. We all had an opportunity to create a space for the world to be present in a whole new and enlightened way. It allowed us to live free of the old concepts that have been handed down generation after generation after generation. In our 'fall from grace,' we reclaimed our grace and are present with it now."

Jesus and the many other Masters involved in Lightstar also came forth with their wisdom. It was clear to all of us that the past six years had been a period of integration on *ALL* levels for everyone involved. It wasn't just about ourselves, but about the whole as well.

As you read these final words about Project Lightstar you may, as we suggested earlier, feel yourself in the energy of this great birthing. We feel as though these past years have been a time of intense integration for many, if not all, Lightworkers. We do not consider ourselves to be the only points of seeding. What took place for those of us directly involved in this project was representative of the enormous strides that Lightworkers everywhere have been making toward the conscious anchoring of light on this planet. We recognize and honor that we are one great spiritual family united in our task.

Toward the end of our reunion, the Masters had this message:

"We bring to you great joy and great love from many Masters, teachers and friends of deeply like heart and mind. We come to be with you now, again, as we were at Lighthouse many years ago.

"This is a time of reunion, where you are gathering your own memories of the time you spent together at Lighthouse. It is an opportunity to appreciate all that you have done since that time.

We ask you to seek your own counsel as to what you feel the purpose of this project was and how it has influenced your life and who you are today, as well as the impact that you consider it to have on your future.

"Two and a half months may have seemed like a very short time to birth yourselves, but you were not 'in time' and you know that. You were in brilliance. You were in a safe harbor of complete and total love. All of us were devoted to you and you were devoted to yourselves. Imagine how aware that can make one! You have seen what love can accomplish when you have witnessed someone basking in it for but a few moments. When you have basked in love yourselves for but a few moments, you have opened, you have deepened, you have surrendered. So, imagine how much opening, how much surrendering you accomplished in a period of two and a half months of pure love. This is why it has been said that you cleared at least a hundred lifetimes in that period.

"Each one of you has deepened greatly. Each one of you has been faced with many, many challenges in the last six years. Each one of you feels very strongly about how you responded to those challenges. We ask you at this time not to pay attention to how you may have felt weak in the face of those challenges, but instead to focus all of your attention on how well and with how much grace you embraced those challenges.

"Your time at Lighthouse was a period when each of you returned to your home planet. You were on Earth and, simultaneously you were traveling the stars. You were vibrating fully in both your physical and your light bodies. The grid work that you picked up for yourselves from your home planet was grounded into your systems during that period at Lighthouse. You experienced yourselves being very present in your physical forms and yet so wide awake on the subtle levels of your Being—more than you had ever been.

"If you look at your experiences there, you will see how true this is. These were not the things that were spoken about, but they were the things that you knew. When your time at Lighthouse was over, you entered your earth arena a completely different person. It was for you to discover how you were going to re-create your life.

"These last six years have not been so much about parts of you surfacing or clearing, as they have been about you rearranging your lives to accommodate and reflect who you truly are *now*. We know there have been times when you have wondered what on earth you were doing, who you were, what happened and where you were going. These questions are important, and yet at the same time, they are quite unimportant because the questions all have the same answer. The answer is *home*. Home, which is now in your heart—your Christ Heart.

"In your heart lies the answer to every single question you have. Remember, you are not on a search. You already *are* the answer. Sit quietly and with gratitude, because you already are where you always wanted to be.

"What we shared at Lighthouse was truly beautiful. The form that encased our experience has now dissolved but the energy of it, the sacredness of it, continues to blossom inside and through you. These past years have been essential in integrating the energy so that your wholeness would be anchored through your bodies, through your actions and into the core crystal of the Earth.

"Now, new choices await each of you—and there are many. But the only important choice is, and always will be, simply choosing God in you. Feel yourselves becoming less and less at the effect of the world and the many choices that it must make, realizing that you are no longer of the mass consciousness. You do not live at that frequency anymore. Therefore the choices people need to make who still live in the arena of mass consciousness are not the same as those you need to make. You can let them have those choices just as you can let yourself have your own.

"You have felt that the greatest struggle you have experienced during these years of integration has been your confusion as to how you fit into the structure of the world at large. Your questions have been, 'Who am I? Where do I fit? Do I belong here?' In truth, your greatest struggle has been with yourself. Your real question has been, 'Will I or won't I let myself *be* here?'

"Each of you already knows inside that your truth, your world, your reality, where you belong and where you fit is right inside of who you truly are—because that is what you have brought to this planet. That is what you awakened in Mount Shasta. It is what you have been learning to accommodate and express ever since. Your integration has been teaching you how to live your sacred Being each moment in the world where you are.

"This task we speak of is your freedom. It is the Christ Consciousness coming alive—the holiest of holiest of holiest in you, living and breathing on planet Earth. Nothing else matters. It is your passionate aliveness expressing in all areas of your life, from the sublime to the mundane.

"So many people speak of the consciousness changing, of windows opening, of impulses being redirected. And what do you think it's all about? It's about everybody exploding into themselves! It's not about something outside; it's about everyone being lit up so brightly inside that they *know* they are free!

"For each one of you, it is time to come face-to-face with yourself as a Master and to own the brilliance of your shining light. Coming to Earth was a very important decision each one of you made. Because you have been here many times before, you gave it a great deal of thought. You asked yourselves, 'Why do I want to come and what do I want to do there?' And you answered, 'I know I have something to give, and I ache to give it. It is my joy to see life come to life. It is my greatest passion to be present at times of birth. I love it. I want to be part of this. I do not care what I have to experience in order to have it, in order to be awake at this birthing. I know what I can contribute, and I am determined to contribute!' This was your heart's desire and this you are fulfilling.

"As you shine your Light so graciously, Life everywhere wants to give back to you. Everywhere, and on every level, you are loved. Your heart needs to be fully open for you to know this and that part is up to you.

"You have infinite passion, each one of you. It is larger than you. But, in order to be alive, to be awake, to be contributing, to be engaged in this passion that you brought with you, you have to be willing to receive it, to breathe it, to live it. You must let go of everything that is unlike it. Do not struggle with this. Give your struggle back to the light because you are not made of that struggle. It is not who you are and you know that. You are fluid and receptive. You are harmony and you are grace.

"Call forth your passion and more of it will be available to you. The more you use, the more you have. Call forth the love in your heart. The more you love, the more love you have. Call forth your freedom. The more you live it, the greater it is. Life is constantly wanting to show you how eager it is to bless you. Bless yourself and you will have opened the way to receive the multitudinous blessings of life around you.

"This reunion is a celebration for all of us. *Open your senses right now and feel the conclusion of Project Lightstar. Experience the final integration right this moment of that pure, most divine energy into the ethers of the consciousness of this planet.*

"We are so grateful to you. You made this seeding possible. There is such love for you of the deepest kind. It is just because you are who you are, and because you have given of the greatness of your Being many times over. If you let us, we will be able to pour our love into you, to touch you, and to do what we can to support you in living your beauty, your brilliance, your shining light.

"Let us join hands now. Christ is joyously born today! This sacred energy has now dispersed itself in the ethers around us so that others, when and as they feel ready, will be able to pluck from the ethers a piece of that crystal and take it into their own hearts to light up the Christ star within themselves.

"This is what you have given to the world. This was the birthing you have supported so beautifully all this time. Know this. Know what a special and sacred gift this is that you have given. Take this truth into your heart right now so that in the months and the years to come you can appreciate the fullness of your gift. You are going to witness many, many people being born into themselves thanks to you. You will see it in the biggest of ways, the smallest of ways and in the most daily of ways. This we guarantee. And, every time you see it, be happy. Be happy for yourself and be happy for those awakening. It is the fulfillment of a dream.

"Your lifetime on this plane is not a lifetime that you will ever consider to be wasted in any way. You'll always look back on it as a very, very special time, a most special incarnation of great light, great love and *great adventure*!

"Honor your greatness now. Understand what your purpose in Project Lightstar has been and acknowledge all that you have gained from it. Always remember what you brought to bear in this and the joy that you experienced in paving the way for others to be free. Truly acknowledge your love, your strength and your steadfastness. Your devotion and love of God is profound. You have demonstrated this with all the grace of your Being. You are indeed a blessing to us all.

"Our gratitude is with you in the deepest way. We will do many, many more things like this in times to come. We are friends of heart forever. Peace."

As we looked back on Lightstar and felt the extraordinariness of its energy, we were touched yet again. After the reunion, we both experienced a dramatic shift in our energy field and knew the integration had been completed. We felt renewed, simplified and grateful. As we ourselves passed into a whole new level of our Mastery, we savored our love with these four Lightstar interns and our love of the Project that had been fulfilled by us all.

As we took note of the rewards and challenges of integration that had been common among us, we could see clearly how the intensity of what we had experienced required six or more years to settle inside us and inside the Earth. Both of us knew from this experience that we were now well-equipped to assist and support others in the integration of light at these refined and activated levels.

What we had all done had taken great heart and great guts. We now moved forward feeling strong, proud and more masterful than ever. Upon this completion, our experience of life had much more "ease" about it. Our foundation was now solid and steady, and we were ready for anything!

Chapter Eight

The Christ Heart

Jesus showed us that *living* our light was possible. He taught us that we could all embody our light if we chose to incarnate upon Earth and claim this as our living reality. As his energy planted these seeds of fulfillment for the future, many of us took notice and began to move toward this goal.

In each of our incarnations since the time of Jesus, we have all been actively building our spiritual fiber to accommodate more and more light so that we could embody it the way Jesus did. In his lifetime, we deified him and believed that our spirit lay in his hands. We believed that he was the Master and we were not.

Now we are realizing that we, too, are God incarnate. It is time for every one of us to enter our own Mastery and find out what this means specifically. It is time for each of us to manifest the gifts we came here to express.

Awakening to the Christ Heart is essentially the transition from fear to love. It means taking ourselves off the wheel of fear and ignorance, and knowing ourselves as the true masters and loving wise ones that we are. In order to do this, we need to trade our ignorance for our inner knowledge, our fear for love, our helplessness for creativity, our hopelessness for passion. The trade needs to be absolute, the commitment total.

Jesus embodied all of this, and so much more. He showed us the "end product" for which we could reach in ourselves. His message to us over and over again was summed up in one word: LOVE.

Love, as we all know, is not just a feeling, an emotion, a connection. It is an electrical vibration, a current of energy that is infinitely powerful. It is the very fabric of the universe in which we live, and of each cell in our body. Through the energy of love, there is nothing that cannot be healed, cleansed, restored or created. In our modern times, we are on the edge of discovering the true power of this energy within our own hearts and hands.

In the last chapter, we spoke much about the Christ consciousness, its birthing at Lighthouse, and its realization into our three-dimensional physical world. We spoke at length about the Christ Heart, the core energy of the Christ consciousness which embraces the values of love, honor, integrity, cooperation, balance and harmony. These ideals are not lofty and beyond our reach—they are the actual qualities of the Christ Heart. They are who we *truly* are.

It is true that these principles have not shown themselves to be the governing values of our planet to date, but they are within the depths of each and every human being. They can and will be brought forward and, as this happens, our Earth will change.

We who have come here at this time are responsible for being the "bridge builders" to this change. We are here at a time of personal and global transformation, a transition from one level of consciousness into another. We are here to bridge the transition from a three-dimensional construct, based on the patriarchal paradigm of parent/child authority and dominion, to a multi-dimensional construct, the Christ Heart reality, which offers a broader field of freedom for all. This new paradigm is neither patriarchal nor matriarchal. Rather, it forges a brand new field of what could be termed "spirituarchal," based on all the values that we associate with love, equality and freedom.

We are each a pioneer in this undertaking. This asks of us that we respond boldly to the reason why we came to Earth in the first place. It demands that we rise to meet our purpose as pioneers and not get lost in the shuffle of confusion and chaos we came here to transform. It demands that we pick ourselves up, pull ourselves out of the muck and mire of mass consciousness, dust ourselves off and restore ourselves to our true knowing of who we are without any veils of illusion blinding us any longer.

Each of us needed to know about the mass consciousness of our time—we needed to feel it, taste it, eat it and drink it thoroughly—so that we could be effective in bridging that consciousness into its new destiny. We immersed ourselves in it to be educated and to clean up any of our own "old business" that needed to be transformed before we could realize the true glory of our light here on Earth. But we are done with our "immersion exercise" now. We must see it for what it has been, bless it for its teachings, and reach now for the power of our light which will infuse and transform us into living, breathing, physically realized, Light Beings. This is why we came. You are reading this book now to be reminded of that fact. It is time to take your greater purpose seriously and do what you need to do to get on with it.

This book is deliberately designed to shake loose the old foundations in you and alert you to the fact that now is the time to take to your new road in a determined and assertive fashion. There are messages in these chapters from all the dimensions of life that are involved in the great lighting of this star and all living forms upon her. Some of these dimensions are represented through the written word and some are not—but their energy is here. There are many "unseen ones" who are witness to what we, the human pioneers, are doing. They are closer than we can imagine, giving their support and cooperation, their love and assistance *in whatever ways we ask of them.*

In previous chapters, we wrote about some of this. But it was just a tiny sampling of the assistance that stands right here for us now. It is important for us to recognize and affirm that we are not here alone. Quite often, people feel so lonely and believe themselves to be—*this is not true.* This loneliness is part of the shroud of ignorance blinding them to their connected-ness, cutting them off from feeling their Source. You must not be a victim of this belief. Open now to acknowledge what you know to be true in your cells—that this planet and every lifeform upon her is *with and for you* in your purpose. Every breathing face of God wants freedom and grace and harmony in this world as much as you do. This is a collective desire. It is a collective yearning. It is a collective reality *that is already manifesting.*

When we came to Earth, we knew that we were coming here as part of a great family system. The structure of Earth is based on cooperative family principles. If you came here wanting a strictly solo journey, you came to the wrong place! The vibration of this planet is the vibration of community, family and co-creation. Acknowledging this will provide you with reinforcement and reassurance that you are not alone in this—and that, yes, you may, and are indeed encouraged to, draw upon resources beyond yourself on this plane in order to manifest a higher reality.

Think about it for a moment. You *need* these other dimensions to bring through the tangible presence of a more evolved consciousness than has existed here to date. You *need* your cosmic family to pull this one off.

Over the years, increasing attention and credence has been given to the intelligence of the Earth and her ability as a viable teacher for us. Workshops, seminars and books have been brought forth from the ethers into physical form to cement our connection with this greater nature intelligence—and there will be more. We have been hearing more and more about our sacred connection with the dolphins and the whales, and how people are being healed by them and inspired by their tremendous intelligence and lightness—and there will be more.

In the last five years, increasing legitimacy has been given to the Angelic realm and all of its intelligence, wisdom and teaching—and this, too, will continue to grow. Soon, as these levels of energy are assimilated and thoroughly absorbed into the physical consciousness, more and more subtle realms of energy will also begin to make their presence known on a mass level.

Why is this? Two reasons. Firstly, that yes, the consciousness has already expanded and the receptivity of the mass consciousness to these subtle levels indicates this. Secondly, it is bringing us to levels of greater wisdom within ourselves as it acts as our mirror and reflection. It is the active and *conscious* integration of our whole, cosmic, universal family demonstrating itself. We are awakening to our sacred oneness with our human, elemental, animal, angelic and star families of light. This is a very beautiful and powerful happening. Seeing this conscious integration gradually occurring around us proves that our purpose is succeeding. And, it is proof that we are joined with many others beyond this planet, beyond our three-dimensional construct, who are here in this evolutionary transformation *with us.*

It is vital that we acknowledge these facts at this time. Vital because we are going to need this support and assistance as we fulfill our greater purposes in being here on Earth. We can label this assistance whatever we choose, but it's all the same principle—that we are reaching for a source of wisdom and love greater than our "limited selves." We are calling upon a higher power that will enable us to manifest our own Christ Heart reality here in the physical plane.

We mentioned earlier about each one of us being a bridge to this new consciousness. As we each more fully embody it, as we each live and breathe our own Christ Heart reality, we emit this new vibration and call it in more closely for others to experience. We add greatly to the pool of possibility for all humans and all lifeforms upon this planet. In our embodiment, the tentacles of the old ways automatically dissolve as they are transformed and swept into the glory of this expanded awareness. In this way everything, including old thought forms, are blessed and healed. Nothing that has ever been created is left out of this resurrection to love. Nothing. If it exists at all, on any level, it is transformed by the power of this love.

The love of the Christ Heart is tremendously powerful, so powerful that it can change an entire global reality. We, who have been mired in the ignorance that has so veiled us to our light, must realize how powerful our true essence is. We cannot, *and must not,* seek to understand it and hold it in direct proportion to what we have known so far. The level of love that we have experienced until now is nothing compared to what is possible within us at our Christ crystal level.

Are we willing to open to this power? Are we willing to do what it takes to know and live this? Are we ready to step up to the plate and take responsibility for our light? It is essential to honestly ask ourselves these questions. Once answered, the reality of what it means to each one of us can then be explored.

Living our Christ Heart in the present state of mass consciousness is by no means an easy feat. This needs to be fully appreciated. The call to make this journey, to feel the glory of your truly awakened, fully realized, Christ Consciousness self in the physical plane, has to come from deep within the heart. It has to be so important and of such priority that all else is consumed by it. This is not to say the rest of your life needs to be put on hold in the face of it. Quite the contrary, as it is a journey that includes all aspects of your expression. Prioritizing it in your daily awareness enables all phases of your life to be blessed and transformed appropriately by this energy. It is a state of mind, an attitude, more than anything else. But a top priority it must be, because without making it *that* important, it will probably not happen for you in this lifetime.

Why do we stress the demands of this journey so much? Well, think about it for a moment. You are taking what has been a predominantly *non-physical,* subtle awareness and literally manifesting it into denser, concrete, physical form. You are birthing yourself from one dimension to another, bringing the fullness of yourself more and more *present.* As you do this, you are bursting open the three-dimensional design that has shaped and dominated your Earth experience for centuries.

As mentioned earlier, by living the reality of your Christ Heart self you are changing not only your own matrix but also the global patterning. In successfully fulfilling your greater purpose, you are shifting an entire global thoughtform of victimization and powerlessness, an entire matrix of fear and limitation, to one of love and harmony. You are dissolving the old patterning just as though it had never existed. Now do you see why we say this is an extraordinary undertaking?

This journey is not an easy one because, frankly, it is not designed to be. It is through its challenges that we grow strong and resilient. It is through its demands that we are squeezed into tight corners so that we will face ourselves and witness the flame of greatness burning within. It is through *walking the journey itself,* through embracing the experience of what life brings to us along its way, that we clear our veils and expand our physical, emotional and mental identities to include the enormous spiritual grace that we have been waiting and longing to retrieve and remember.

This journey is meant to be an experience that increases our spiritual fiber, adding strength and stamina to our system so that we are then capable of bringing through the vastness of our Being. If it all just happened in an instant without us strengthening both our ability to assimilate this energy and our understanding of its purpose and how to express it, it would be like putting a sophisticated race car engine in an old VW bug—too much power without the body to sustain it.

We need to start thinking of ourselves as elite athletes. Just as they must train and condition their bodies and minds to perform at top levels of their game, so must we condition our bodies, minds and emotions to align with the intelligence of our spirits. We, too, must be willing to be vigilant in our efforts to nurture, support and discipline ourselves, as needed, on our path of embodying our Mastery.

As you each know, you have free will. It is up to you how fully you participate in your life and what level of consciousness you choose to radiate. When you choose, however, to go for the highest available within you, in your reaching you must be willing to stand fully by yourself to get there. *No-one* is going to do it for you. You can be supported and assisted by your friends, in human form as well as those in other dimensions, but the actual work of your journey is your very own. It is your own sacred masterpiece unfolding and you are its artist and caretaker.

Know that this will most likely be a challenging and muscle-building time. Much has been written and shared about the wonders of the spiritual journey and, of course, this is the absolute truth. Certainly we have also demonstrated our share of this in these pages. If it wasn't as rewarding as it is, we wouldn't even embark upon it. But there is also the other side of the mountain and this needs so desperately to be addressed.

Yes, there is likelihood that you will meet some opposition on your journey. It will take many different forms and faces. Our reason for discussing this is not to set it up for this to happen, but to prepare you and give you some tools to assist you. Given the nature of your task, preparation can only help, not hinder, as with Olympic skiers who must learn how to "right" themselves when they slip on an icy spot during a race. Who's to say what the precise conditions of the snow will be and what this will demand of them? Will they know enough to shift their balance in the right way, or roll through a fall without getting hurt? They need to prepare for these contingencies ahead of time so that they'll have the best chances of winning.

In our years of traveling our spiritual journey and in our work of facilitating others, we have seen that it is predominantly the lack of understanding of what is happening at different stages of this journey that has created the greatest distress and disillusionment. How sad it is that people would reach a place within themselves where they feel they need to give up on their spiritual quest. After all, what else is there once the glories of our spirits have been tasted and touched? Everything else pales by comparison. But what do you do when the going seems to be so tough that it seems easier to quit? How can we understand this process more fully, its joys, its demands and how it will change us?

These are some of the questions to which we will be offering answers in this chapter. But first, it will be helpful for us to deeply reconnect with our desire to make our spiritual journey. Defining exactly why you feel this is important to you will help ignite your excitement and fortify your sense of purpose so that the energy of this reality becomes even more tangible to you.

As we have said, we are carving a brand new path for ourselves and for others to follow in our wake. This is something for which we can deeply appreciate ourselves. We are endeavoring to live a level of consciousness which has not been known *en masse* on this planet for a very long time, if ever. Through our own emergence, we are literally forging a new race of humankind. We are the pioneers and we have what it takes to do this. If we didn't, we wouldn't have even thought about it in the first place.

WHY IS LIVING THE CHRIST HEART IMPORTANT?

It is time now to examine this question in a personal and intimate way. What *exactly* would it look like for *you* to be living every moment of every day from the energy of your Christ Heart? What exactly does this mean to *you*? How would *you* feel and what would *you* be doing if you were living as this fully self-realized person? In what ways would *you* and your life be any different? Give yourself a few moments to reflect on these questions. Give yourself a chance to thoroughly imagine it.

Getting in touch with how this would be for you connects you deeply with your inner yearnings to manifest this reality, inspiring you and empowering you to do so. It helps it all become less and less of a dream and more and more of your concrete, viable reality. It reminds you that, in coming to Earth to serve a greater purpose, you are at the center of that service. *You* get to benefit first and foremost. The Earth and all of us around you get the overflow. What a wondrous happening!

We asked Jesus to describe the Christ Heart:

"Everyone has a Christ Heart. It is not the three-dimensional human heart which only knows itself in terms of its feelings and emotions. It is the larger, truer, deeper heart—the sacred heart that lies within your human heart, waiting patiently. Your Christ Heart is a heart which is not in service to self, but to God and the greater good of all. It is waiting for you to reach deeply into it and ask it to come forth. When it does, the three-dimensional definition of your heart shatters and is replaced by a sensation and knowing that is far, far greater than you've ever imagined possible. It brings you overflowing confidence, strength, understanding and true abiding love. The sacred heart, your Christ Heart, is already fully formed and firmly connected with the purity and sacred substance of all of life.

"Your Christ Heart *knows*—it listens, it loves, it is endlessly compassionate, it forgives, it touches, it understands, it sees, it hears, it cares.

"Stand aside from how you have viewed yourselves in the past and invite this glorious seed to shine forth and show you who you *really* are—how much you truly love and how much you deeply care. Let it show you that you are loved by others, loved by nature, loved by all of us on all levels—passionately.

"In this knowing, in this direct sensory feeling experience, you will surrender. It is the natural way of things. You will shed and let go of all of your hardness as your armor crumbles to the ground around you. You cannot maintain such weight and exist in such light at the same time.

"Humankind has clothed itself in a cold, uncaring darkness. It has shrouded its heart. No more! The cover is lifting, the armor is cracking, the inner light is beginning to pierce through the outer shield of ignorance. *Darkness will be no more!*

"Something stays cold until it is warmed. Darkness exists until light dawns. The human heart is closed until it is cared for. Make no judgement about where there appears to be no light, no warmth, no love—simply know that it has not yet been touched. Touch it and make the difference. Touch it and bring light to it. Touch it and bring its light to life. Touch it, not with effort, but only with gentle love and understanding.

"Your Christ Heart knows and understands these things. It is its love pouring forth—uplifting, including, connecting. Your Christ Heart is your loving and caring—uniting, cleansing and birthing you as the innocent Master that you are.

"Long for this love and caring no more. It is within you, to have fully and consistently. Know this, and in your knowing, share it with the world."

In these words, you can feel the power and the grace that we each hold in our hearts. You can feel your own desire to know this on a daily basis, consciously, and to see exactly how its expression will alter your life and the lives of those you touch. How much can it change you? What could this look like? How deeply can it make a difference? Are you willing to find out?

We spoke earlier in this chapter about the challenges many of us face along this path and it is for this reason that it is especially important to be clear, very clear, about *why* you have chosen to make this journey. Yes, you know it is your soul's purpose, but what about your daily heart and mind?

When things feel wonderful, you won't wonder why you wanted to be free. You will be basking in your feelings of openness and delighted by your love of life coursing joyously through you. You will be grateful for your sense of belonging, and you will give freely of this warmth to all you meet. You will know that the joys of being centered in your Christ Heart are innumerable, that they are as exquisite as you can imagine and receive.

But how will you feel about this journey when it asks that you truly stretch, let go and travel beyond your usual boundaries of comfort? Then will you still remember the joy of it? Will you still be clear about why you wanted this so much? Perhaps you will. But then again, if you're like most of us, the mind can have an extremely short memory when its own terms are not being met!

It is precisely for these more demanding times that it is very helpful to have already defined why this journey is important to you. It is even more helpful to have a written list of these reasons tucked away for reference. It may sound corny now, but you'll be really glad that you have it later. There is nothing like being able to read something that will inspire and lift you up in times of need. Why not make that inspiration be *directly relevant to you* and what you are doing day by day?

We encourage you to sit down right now and start making your list. Begin by writing down all the reasons that pop instantly into your head without analyzing any of them. Notice if and how any of these reasons speak to your heart, your mind or both. Notice if they are more generalized or more specific.

To help jog your thoughts even further, we have put together a list of some of the exquisite rewards of the Christ Heart journey. In looking at this list, consider how it can be translated into practical terms in your everyday experience. Take the energy of the Christ Heart and move it from its expanded state and bring it into something directly useful and pragmatic. Some of the questions we have added in each category will show you what we mean.

In listing some of the benefits in this direct and simple way, it becomes apparent how fulfilling it can be to engage our Christ Heart. We saw and felt Jesus living it and we were deeply moved. We can be equally as magnificent if we are willing to engage ourselves at this level.

These rewards are not realized overnight, but they do begin to become apparent rather quickly into the journey. Stating them here is designed to motivate and inspire you. Use them as further reference for defining your own reasons. We all know that if we can expect something great as a result of our labor, we will be more inclined to persevere and urge ourselves forward.

1. *You find personal freedom.* You gain it not because someone outside of you gives it to you, but because you take it for yourself. It has always been there regardless of your beliefs and those of the world in which you live. Now you know you can have it. It is all your very own.

    Personal freedom means something different to everyone. Bring it out of the conceptual realm and define exactly what it means to you in practical, meaningful terms. Where have you felt enslaved or imprisoned by others or by "the system?" To whom have you given power of authority over you? If you want to be free, free yourself!

2. *You gain love instead of fear.* Through your sacred journey of self-realization, you walk completely away from the wheel of fear and everything associated with it. You get to be released from all "fear bondage"—past, present and future. Think about the fears that currently run you and imagine how it would be to not have them anymore. Who would you be? How would you behave? What would you express that you have been holding back? And to whom?

3. *You discover trust and synchronicity.* You stop struggling and pushing. You find yourself cascading joyously in the natural flow of life. Think about the areas in your life where you tend to push. Think about all the things that you try to "make happen." How would your life be different if you simply trusted? In your "allowing," how would this make you feel?

4. *You discover eternal life.* You no longer see yourself limited to this incarnation in the body. Instead, you discover yourself as a soul on its path of divine evolution, taking many forms, but always with a consciousness that is alive and free. Think about having no fear or tightness about death. How that would change you? What would you do differently? Say differently? And to whom?

5. ***You gain full knowledge and power of your light.*** You are no longer depressed, suppressed or repressed. You are shining and purposeful, vibrant and clear. How would this change what you do and how you perceive yourself? What about your self-esteem and self-respect? What about your feelings of fulfillment and self-worth? What about your gratitude to your Source?

6. ***You are at peace.*** You gain the bliss of total alignment and harmony with your Self. In this alignment, you have health and wealth on all levels. You have the enthusiasm and stamina to express your purpose. You gain the joy and relief of exercising your muscles on all levels as you express the full range of your creative passion. Think about how this would change your concept of "job" or "career." Wouldn't it become "expressing your passion and ability" rather than "making a living"?

7. ***You are aware of and appreciate your beauty—and the tremendous beauty everywhere.*** You see beyond the mind's eye, hear beyond the mind's ear, feel beyond the mind's senses. Through these essential openings, you gain access to the intelligence of all life. You gain a wider expanse of creative possibility than you have ever dreamed could exist. How would this change your opinion of how beautiful, how wise, how inspired and inspiring you are? How would this change what you have perceived to be the limits of your intelligence and ability to create? What would you do differently?

8. ***You more fully understand yourself and others.*** Your heart has opened to you and to them. You are able to see the "bigger picture" behind the smaller dramas that we all experience. This changes how you relate to yourself as well as your family, friends and whoever you meet. You are no longer afraid to connect in deep and intimate ways. You are no longer afraid to be yourself. You are no longer afraid to let others grow on their own path. You truly get to live—and let live. How would this change how you treat yourself? How would

this change how you treat your father, mother, husband, wife, significant other? How would this change how you treat your children? How would this change how you treat your friends, your co-workers and your acquaintances?

9. ***You witness and appreciate the difference you make in other peoples' lives.*** You understand and respect your contribution to the whole. You understand your role as an equal player and you love it. It is wondrously fulfilling. You find it exciting to live, to learn, to make a difference. You are empowered—and empowering. How does this make a difference in your day?

10. ***You know you are God.*** This is not an ego trip talking. It is a deeply inspiring and strengthening truth. Knowing it brings endless joy, comfort, peace and tranquility to every second of your life. It enables you to feel really good about taking your rightful place in the universe amongst all of God's many forms and faces. It brings you endless energy and gratitude for every moment of life. It makes you laugh from your belly because you know it's true. How does softening into this truth feel?

In reading over these categories, simply notice what thoughts come into your awareness as you read them and how any of them may have moved you. As you reflect, the energy will open the way for you to receive information from an even deeper level inside of you about your reasons for living the Christ Heart.

When you feel ready, we invite you to sit back and relax. We invite you to go deeper inside of yourself to feel the stir of your spirit. Because your mind is so used to thinking three-dimensionally instead of multi-dimensionally, you need to assist it in engaging this expanded reality more fully. You can do this now by inviting your spirit to show you how this could truly look and feel through your physical body, thoughts, feelings and actions. Know that your spirit is eager to give you any additional motivation it can to help you persevere on this journey. This is one of the ways it can do that, so why not invite it to do so now?

When you are ready, close your eyes and place your attention inside your heart. Feel your simple love and caring that vibrates there. Feel your gratitude towards yourself for the fact that you even *want* to open, that you even want to be more fully you. Feel your excitement about your inner senses coming alive, making it easier for you to feel a part of life everywhere around you. Feel your excitement about being thoroughly joyous and finding out what *your* true freedom means to *you*. Feel how excited you are about having an experience of yourself that is exquisite and satisfying right down to the very tips of your toes.

As you connect more deeply with yourself in this quiet way, ask your spirit to speak to you. Ask your spirit to clarify even more fully the reasons you are on this journey. Invite your spirit to show you, through your inner senses, how it will feel and look for you to be living on Earth right now as a self-realized, Christ-hearted Being. Ask it to fill you full on every level with the sensations of this. Soften and open to receive your spirit teaching you now.

As you continue to hold yourself in the trusting, gentle energy of invitation and receptivity, notice whatever you sense, see or feel. Notice what you hear and smell. Notice any physical sensations, any emotions, any clear thoughts. Be aware—making no decisions or judgements.

Write down your impressions. This is an experience for you to open to the truth of this reality emerging through you. This is a time to be receptive and welcome whatever comes to you. Don't get upset if it isn't all crystal clear. Instead, focus more on the sensations of what you *are* feeling. Probe your experience and be more attentive to the subtleties. If you find that not much happens, do not be disappointed. Something has definitely shifted inside of you, and the information will most probably pop into your psyche at a later time. In any case, this is a process which we encourage you to repeat as often as you like.

During the course of this exercise, you can also ask your spirit specific questions about direct areas of interest and concern in your life, and how these would be changed by living your Christ Heart. Ask about your specific areas of need—your family, your health, your job, your finances, etc. Listen and receive whatever impressions your spirit gives you. Write them down and add them to your growing list of the rewards of this journey.

By inviting your spirit to engage with you, you are supporting yourself in living your Christ Heart more fully and easily. In so doing, you are being a student of your spirit. You are being educated, nourished and infused with your own greater wisdom.

In asking the questions and feeling the answers, you can define more and more clearly the gains and advantages of living your Christ Heart. You can feel the potential changes it will bring as you grow stronger and more centered in it. Do whatever you can to bring it into your physical arena more and more consciously. This is where your questions, your imagination, your thinking and feeling processes can really help you to *anchor* this energy more tangibly in your awareness and in your life. Just as a seed needs time and nurturing to sprout and develop into a plant, you need the same regarding coming into your Christ Heart. *Be patient and trusting with yourself.*

As you define your reasons in your mind and on paper, be as specific as possible. The more concrete and tangible the better. All of this will only serve to motivate and inspire you, and to bring the reality in more effectively. Read these reasons over and reflect upon them whenever you get stuck, disillusioned, lazy or simply forgetful. Decide ahead of time what you will do in those instances. Will you go to sleep, forget or go away? Or will you remind yourself why you have chosen this path? Remember your reasons and keep them close in your heart on a daily basis. Affirm and re-affirm them to yourself. Reflect on them as you go about the routines of your day. Let them swell and ripen in your mind. Taste them in your mouth. Water them in your heart. Feel them in your body. Let yourself have this reality because it is right here for you.

As you are already aware, consciousness on this planet is expanding at a very rapid rate. The train is already moving—and moving very fast! It's far easier simply to get on the train and let it carry you instead of wishing you were on it while still being back at the station. The Christ Heart is the way of our future. It is for us to start living it now. Don't wait to be chosen. Simply choose yourself!

Whatever aspects of your life and conditioning have taught you that you were not good enough to have something as wonderful as this, bless them now and let them go. Be the one who walks off the "wheel of fear" and decides that this is no longer the veil that will blind you or the illusion that will run you.

Chapter Nine

Moving Through Interference

"There is an open field available within each of you wherein you feel and grasp the truth of your Being. In this field, you are not engaged in struggle with your mind or your heart. You can feel your oneness, you can see it within the grace of your body, you can feel it vibrating through your awakened senses.

"You are open and clear. You are listening, attentive and taking action upon what you hear. In this open, clear field there is no interference. There are no past and no future expectations to bind you. You are peaceful in your mind and heart, overcome with joy at the true recognition of your freedom.

"Recognize that there is this still, clear place in you. If ever you meet struggle within, if ever you meet interference along your way, reach for this place. Come into it. Know its sensations so thoroughly that this is where you return, again and again. In this haven of love and tranquility, all else is transformed and you are restored to your peace. It enfolds you so fully that this is all you know."

— Master Jesus

One of the major challenges we encounter as we embody our Christ Heart more fully is learning to stay clear and true to who we really are at all times and in all situations. To help ourselves do this, it is also important to learn how to recognize and transform interference.

Anything that impedes or blocks our process of self-realization is interference. It can either be from within us, or it can be what we allow to come in from the outside and affect us in non-supportive ways. As we each forge a new path of love, joy and freedom in this world, we are threatening the old thoughtforms both on personal and collective levels. As bridge builders to the new, it is not unusual to feel this pressure of the old wanting to hold us back. The more we understand this interference, the better we can manage ourselves in the face of it.

As the word interference implies, it is *enter-fear-ence*—fear coming in which we allow to disturb our peace and progress of physically engaging the tremendous scope of love and creativity emerging through our Christ Heart. The energy of interference can feel just like fear itself or it can be any quality of emotion that we lump under the heading of "negative feelings," i.e. pain, sadness, unworthiness, insecurity, loneliness, self-doubt, worry, obsession, turmoil, anger, resentment, confusion, overload, etc. Fear is the generator of all of these feelings—it just wraps itself in different packages. We each pick the ones that best describe our internal experience.

Imagine that you are like a clear signal on a radio; interference is like the static that comes in and distorts your clear connection with yourself. This energy of interference can come from a variety of different sources. For example, it can simply be negative energy from other people, even those who are well-meaning and who "love" us but are threatened by our changes. It can be negative energy from places where we spend a lot of time, or sometimes even places where we are just passing through. It can be negative messages that we take in through newspapers and magazines or that are blasted across the airwaves of TV, radio and, most recently, through the computer—the Internet. What makes it interference versus just "energy out there" is *what we do with it.*

If we feel the energy as something that we know is not our own, then it can be useful in providing us with information about what is around us. But, if we take it in and *identify* it as *ours* when it really isn't, then it becomes something that can literally upset or impede our progress. It is like damming up a river that is designed to flow freely, or dropping anchor on a moving boat. It can slow us down, halt us altogether, and even make us start going backwards, depending upon how much we buy into it.

The following example of interference, at its most basic level, is one to which we can all relate. We all know the feeling of walking into someone's home and feeling welcomed, warm and invited. It makes us want to share ourselves openly. Conversely, we also know the feeling of walking into someone else's home and feeling the opposite—uninvited, closed, negative, protective, possibly even fearful. This, of course, makes most of us contract inside and shut down.

To take this a step further, think of a time when you went to a party and it felt really good to be there. The energy of the place and the people was inviting and joyful. Naturally, you had a great time. Now, think of another time when you went to a party, and before you went, you felt great. This time, once you arrived, it didn't feel so good to be there. It may have even felt horrible. You may have begun to question yourself. This is where, with a shred of self-doubt, you suddenly think to yourself, "Oh, what's wrong with me tonight? Everyone else seems to be having a fine time. Why am I not having fun? It must be me."

At this point, you have assumed that the discomfort is all your own. You have taken the "problem" as yours, instead of reading the energy of the people and the place. If you knew you were feeling great before you got there, then it's not you at all but the situation you just walked into. Certainly, many of us have had this experience.

Interference is the intrusion of our personal and collective thought patterns that maintain we are separate from our Source. In order for us to fully appreciate the task of returning to our truth of oneness, it helps to acknowledge the huge disparity between the belief systems we are leaving behind and those we are now choosing for ourselves. They are, in fact, the opposite of one another. When you see this clearly, it explains exactly why so many people have moments of intense conflict during the course of their journey of liberation.

Let us examine this more closely now. Imagine that from one corner of a stage, you hear the voice of the "old, limited consciousness" while from the other corner you hear the voice of the "new, expanded consciousness." From the old corner, we hear, "I am weak, I am a sinner, I am unworthy, I am small."

In the opposite corner we hear, "I am a Master, I am universal, I am multi-dimensional, I am vast." From the old corner, "I am afraid, I am limited." From the other corner, "I am love, I am free." From the old corner, "This lifetime is the only one there is." From the opposite corner, "This incarnation is just one of many." From the old corner, "When my body dies, that's the end." From the new corner, "The death of my physical form simply marks another transition of my life; I am eternal."

Look at the polarities here. Perhaps it will help you to have greater compassion for yourself as you transition from one system of belief to another. It is vitally important to grasp that these two belief systems are not the same. They are not even in agreement. As you will see later in this chapter, the expanded Christ consciousness can embrace the limited, fear consciousness and, in so doing, dissolve and transform it. But, the fear consciousness cannot and will not ever embrace the Christ consciousness, not because it doesn't want to, but because it is simply not designed to do so. It is like a computer that isn't programmed to accept that information. It isn't programmed to go beyond limited survival.

Understanding that there is a wide field of disparity between our conditioned minds and our divine truth enables us to see how large the window is through which interference can enter. Obviously, the more solidly embedded we are in our new consciousness and our intrinsic trust of ourselves, the narrower the doorway through which interference can come at all.

Wherever it comes from and whatever form it takes, it is ultimately up to us whether we let interference disturb our lives and our journey of freedom. Contrary to how it sounds, as well as how it often feels, we are not its victim. Interference can only affect us to the degree that it stimulates fear already residing in us. It is important to be clear about the fact that, ultimately, it is our own limiting thoughtforms that enable interference to touch us. If we didn't have them, there would be nothing for the interference to latch onto. It is precisely these thoughtforms that we need to transform; and ironically, it is through the gifts of interference that we will, in fact, find our way to do this.

As we said, interference is like static in our signal. When we are in its midst, it can sometimes feel like a fog of confusion that prevents us from seeing clearly what we need, while at other times it feels like an inner raging battle. Push and pull. Up and down. In and out. Yes and No. Light and dark. It is the tug of war between our old and new mind. It is our small selves wanting to hold us back in the face of our expanding momentum. And as always, it is the strong one that prevails.

In helping ourselves to understand and minimize the effects of interference in our lives, we must first place our journey of enlightenment in its proper perspective. It must be clearly understood that this journey is the journey of spirit. It is *not* the journey of *human* embracing spirit, but rather *spirit* becoming *humanized*. There is a difference here. The former is a three-dimensional construct, the latter clarifies that it is an overlay template being "physicalized." Knowing this keeps us, the travelers, at a much higher pitch of awareness, enabling us to see interference as it is coming into us and being able to step aside saying, "This is not me. I will not be daunted by this."

We asked Jesus what he wanted to say about interference:

"The energy of interference, no matter what form it takes, can confuse you on your path and purpose. Take your understanding now and use it like an arrow to pierce through that confusion and restore yourself to the sunlit clarity of your pathway.

"Every day, shake loose the strongholds of past conditioning upon you. Each and every morning as you awaken, shake your body and your mind so that those barnacles from the past rattle themselves off you completely. Do not buy into thoughtforms which would convince you that you are too small, too insignificant or too unworthy to hold heaven in your physical hands. Do not be deluded into thinking that this reality is only for those who have 'reached perfection.'

"Where can you find your peace within the chaos of your life? Right here, right now. Put all the chaos aside. Return to your still place within and listen to the quiet that permeates you. What looks like chaos is nothing more than fear trying to make you believe that you cannot find your way. Step aside and let your past identity of ignorance slide right by you. See that you are not filled with confusion, but with light. Allow the sun of your Being to lift the fog of your old beliefs and evaporate them into thin air. Do not be daunted by these old belief systems. They are small, so small, compared to the greatness of who you are. Use your greatness now to clear your way.

"It is essential that you take responsibility for your part in the dance with interference. Holding on to limiting beliefs draws it to you. *Release your hold on the old.* Know that you are not this now. You are clear, a virgin plate, a brand new intelligence asserting yourself into the realm of the physical world. In so doing, you expand your humanness and light it up.

"Interference is nothing more than the pledge of the past to repeat itself. But you are not the past. You are the now! Break new ground. Establish the future right here and now!"

Often in our work, we have heard people say, "I was doing so well and then suddenly I regressed. I felt like I had taken ten steps backwards and I was deeply disappointed in myself. It made me wonder, 'Can I even do this? Am I capable?' "

This is interference at work. Inside these experiences, you will find the smallness of your belief system vigorously asserting itself. What it is saying will depend entirely upon where your own particular "weak areas" are. In other words, it will trip you up at your Achilles Heel.

Here are some examples: If you tend to worry a lot about other people, it will distract you by bringing the multitudes into your life to worry about. If you tend to be a busy person who has precious little time for yourself, it will distract you into greater and greater "busy-ness." If you tend to compare yourself to others, it will drive you crazy measuring yourself against everyone and everything. If you tend to harbor grudges, it will bring you a truck-load of things to feel ripped off about. If you tend to hide behind getting sick, it will make you feel even more sick. If you tend to get easily overwhelmed, it will over-stimulate you until you think you're ready for the nut house.

Interference is simply energy that attaches itself to your "issues." It comes in through these weak areas of your system, exaggerating your issues so you think they are much bigger than they really are. By doing this, you become so consumed and pre-occupied with them that your energy is no longer available for your positive flow and creative movement. As soon as you stand back, assess the situation, and realize that things are way out of their normal proportion, you can rest assured that you are experiencing interference. At this point, retrace your steps and check to see what issues have been stimulated in you and how—then release them. As a result, the interfering energy simply dissolves and you find that you are back on course with your clear signal restored.

The key to recognizing interference is to always give yourself the benefit of the doubt and not assume that what you are feeling in those moments is *only* your own "stuff." If you know yourself well enough, then you already know where your issues lie and how deep they run. In fact, you have probably already worked through them many times over! You will soon be thoroughly acquainted with the feeling of when it is simply your own issue versus the exaggerated form which interference brings.

As we explore interference, we end up discovering it is a great teacher. Its gifts are primarily two-fold. First, it highlights the weak areas in our systems, illuminating our faulty thought patterns so we can change them. Second, it forces us to reach deep within to draw up those qualities of energy in us that will transform these prior "weaknesses." It leads us directly to those beliefs that are not in alignment with who we are, thereby offering us the choice of transforming them into thought patterns consistent with our higher purpose.

Interference, by the discomfort it causes us, can bring us to this choice point—a choice of empowerment instead of defeat. It challenges us, "Are you going to let me interfere with you, maybe even cripple you in your journey? Or will you believe in yourself enough to overcome me?" In response to this question, in response to our desire to be free, we reach down into our depths and discover our strength within. We find out that "hidden in our weak areas" lies our true strength, our Mastery. We are forced to *embody* this energy in order to expand beyond the ability of interference to hamper us. It makes us *become* our true strength in every cell of our consciousness, thus fortifying our newfound design and belief system. It pushes us beyond its illusionary limits into firmly establishing our new field of freedom.

In the final analysis, you can see that interference is not here to dismantle us, but to fortify us. It is through these obstacles that we gain our greatest clarity about ourselves, how we have been believing and worshiping false beliefs and values, and who we really are in our ability to embody and live our greatness. It prompts us to constantly affirm: "I am bigger than this," and, in so doing, this becomes the antidote. We grow beyond the smallness in ourselves, and inevitably prove that this statement is true. As we grow stronger and more masterful in ourselves, interference no longer touches us. *We discover we have outgrown it*—it was simply another learning stage through which we passed. In our strengthening, we discover that no one and nothing is more powerful than we are—such is the magnitude of our love and spiritual fortitude.

Jesus elaborated:

"The main point I want to impress is that interference is actually very, very small and impotent in the face of who you are. It is only the power of your beliefs and the fear of fear that allows it to be alive at all. If you had no fear, if you truly knew how fear-less you are, there would be no such thing as interference. If you did not question your worthiness, if you did not buy into the fact that you even *think* you are unworthy, there would be no way of tripping you up. Because, in truth, there is not an unworthy cell in your Being. So why believe an untruth? Why continue to believe things that are not accurate about you? If you didn't, your greatness would so illuminate your mind that you would bow down in the face of your very self with joy and gratitude.

"You see, interference is an illusion. It is a ruse and only you can decide how long and far you will go along with it."

As our love expands, it dissolves our fear. We become less afraid of fear and more confident in our ability to understand it and transform it. Typically, we have been afraid of fear. It is the only energy in the universe that can cause us to be afraid. It is the only energy with this property in it. It has been said, "there is nothing to fear but fear itself," and this is the truth.

After many years of exploring our own personal fears in different ways, the two of us became curious about the power of this energy. We wondered, "What really is this fear thing anyway? Beyond how we react to it, succumb to it and overcome it, what essentially is it? How is it that there can be an energy that is so intimidating that we give our power to it? What is all this about?"

If given a voice, we wanted to see what this interfering energy might say about the transformation that is happening on our planet. After all, since it is about transforming the wheel of fear, we felt this energy would have something to say. Refreshingly, this is what the voice of fear told us:

"I am the energy of archaic memories, archaic thought systems and beliefs in the disconnectedness and selfishness of the human being. I am fabricated out of untruths, experiences that have been misunderstood and misinterpreted through time.

"I have served you in many ways, one of which is to prevent you from coming forth with your brilliance until such time as you were ready to support yourself in this expression. I have interfered with you many times and made it difficult, if not impossible, for you to be free of constraint. I was protecting you—just as you asked me to. I was serving your notion that you needed this. I was fulfilling the illusion that you helped to create. As long as you believe you are helpless and small, I will be there to keep you corralled and reinforce your belief that this is true.

"I was created out of survival. I am based on the territorial notion that there is not enough to go around, that I must protect my own in order to survive at all. I am the bare bones of human existence without the refinement of love and caring.

"Love is not in my vocabulary. If you wish me to learn about it, you must teach it to me. In truth, however, I am powerless in its wake. You can annihilate me with your love.

"Feel free to annihilate me so that I may dissolve into the great wave of oneness. This may surprise you—but I want this. Would this not be a desirable experience for me to have, just as it would be for you?

"Sometimes, you may experience me as not wanting this. That is only because it is my nature to rear my head in protection of what I am, what I know. This is my purpose and I do it well. I can make you forget who you are and why you are even alive. I can tear you down until you are weak on your knees offering yourself up to me in sacrifice. I can make you believe you are in my power. But you can far outsmart me. Your true spirit is far too great a match for me. You have the power of love that makes me melt. In it, I no longer exist as fear but as love and compassion united in oneness.

"No longer see me as a 'monster.' Do not give me attributes of strength that I do not possess because, in truth, love is far stronger than I and will always win. Know that I will fight you for sure, because that is all I know. I seek to preserve myself and grow, just as you do. But count on one thing: In the throes of love, I lose all potency. It is your choice what you energize.

"Why do I want to die, you ask? It is not death, it is melting into the One. It is my rightful transformation, just as yours is your own. Love me. I am ready and, believe it or not, willing. Transform me with your love, and I will turn into celebration for your freedom."

From this information, you can see how fear has served us all in our limited views of ourselves. As we expand our perception of ourselves and embrace our true nature, we can also see that there is a way through fear, and that fear itself, once transformed, can and will give us even greater powers of love and healing. This is the dissolution of the wheel of fear into the matrix of love and freedom.

In truth, we are all fear-less. As we realize this, the depth of our compassion increases dramatically and the powerful effects of our love reach further and further afield. We are far beyond the "survival game." Our arena of living has now entered the realms of true and satisfying co-creatorship. In this arena, we know our freedom is real and abiding—and we don't have to keep proving it over and over again. From this position of deep spiritual fortitude and trust, we are now clear and graceful agents of Divine Power.

Chapter Ten

Living the Christ Heart

"What's going to strengthen you on this journey?

"THE ABSOLUTE REALIZATION, ACCEPTANCE AND FULL UNHESITATING EMBRACE OF YOUR INNER KNOWING THAT THE CHRIST HEART IS ALREADY HERE AND POSSIBLE WITHIN YOU RIGHT NOW. YOUR FREEDOM IS HERE NOW. IT IS WAITING FOR YOU!

"Your desire to expand in your consciousness lies deep in your heart. I see it shining brightly. Open to your heart now, allowing the Christ crystal lying dormant there to be instantly ignited and activated. As you live and breathe this essence, it will anchor itself more and more firmly into your physical reality. Trust and know this. Follow your heart.

"First, however, you must dismantle the old grid by shedding the old baggage before the new rays of light can shine through you. At every turn, be open-hearted and open-minded, receptive to God's lead and direction. Constantly endeavor to live according to the wisdom of your spirit, not the terms put forth by your conditioned mind. Trust yourself. Open."

— Master Jesus

As we said previously, there are no reference manuals on how to live this new matrix of reality. We know we can have it, but exactly how do we go about living it? Below, we discuss a number of steps regarding the journey of embracing and living the Christ Heart. This information is gleaned from our own experience and from our work with others. You may recall how the four interns from the Lightstar project gracefully went through these steps during their time at Lighthouse and afterwards.

Although most of the points we make here have already been covered throughout this book, we felt it would be helpful to compile them altogether in a framework that would serve as a "road map." Even though this journey is unique to everyone, there are some commonalities we have observed over the years that, put together, allow us to gain perspective. This helps us better understand what is taking place through our liberation process.

None of these steps is written in stone; there are always variations and exceptions to every rule. We share our observations simply as "pointers along the path" in the hopes that they will ease your way should you encounter similar experiences. Although these "steps" are presented in sequential order, keep in mind that this metamorphosis is not a linear process, but rather a fluid motion which weaves in and out of itself. Each one of these steps may continue throughout our lives, and each one will periodically overlap another. As we all know, our evolution is continually awakening us to new realms of ourselves.

1. YEARNING

You hear the call deep within. Your heart aches with a longing for more. Your Christ seed wants to burst forth and emerge with brilliance. You want this brilliance, this newness of life.

You're aching to bring this light into your life—to experience God in human form, to sing with the angels in their gardens, to see the beauty of the colors beyond the human eye, to feel your own closeness with Creation and the God that made you. You yearn to be connected with God and with all of life everywhere—to feel safe, loved and comfortable here. You yearn to demonstrate your deep caring and your tremendously creative abilities which are inherent within you.

The inner restlessness you feel needs to be calmed. But before the calm is the "storm of passion" that is your yearning. It is no mistake that you feel so restless. Something triggers your desire, and it is like adding fuel to a fire. It could be a book, a person or an experience of your own. It could be a so-called "tragedy"—death or illness of someone close, your own illness, a divorce or loss of a job. It is your *gift* even though you may not see it that way initially. And when its time has come, watch out! Your heart opens and your mind starts to yield to your heart and your spirit.

2. REACHING FOR IT

You sense you are able to make a difference here—to bring life to this great planet and to join with the heavens through her. "But how?" you ask yourself. Your spirit answers, "By uniting with your greatness. By joining with God. By lighting your Christ Heart."

You know it is here now, waiting for you. It is as easily available as going to the supermarket. It only requires that you know this, that you *reach for it within, embrace its reality* and get on with the task of integrating it into your three-dimensional and multi-dimensional life.

It is what you have longed for. This is now possible and *available* to you. You reach for it, you persevere and you embrace this crystal within your own heart. It is yours, and your time is now.

3. LETTING GO

In your embrace of your Christ Heart within, your life starts to reorganize itself. This is simply the way of things. Nature shows us how this is so. Everything has its season and purpose, and everything is in a state of constant change. You are the same.

You find yourself shedding the old coats of armor that have kept you bound to fear and ignorance, even though you thought they protected you. You find yourself "standing naked before God." You joyously discard all that is not in accordance with the Christedness you are embracing.

You are making way for the new. You suddenly find yourself not being stimulated or "turned on" by the same things, the same situations, the same people. Nothing has changed but you. You know it's time to let go.

You realize that letting go has been such a misunderstood aspect of our evolvement. It is not just for the sake of releasing. Its main purpose is realignment with your true self, your Christ

Consciousness, and bringing this to bear in all aspects of your life. It is a most positive step.

You reflect on the fact that we haven't been taught or trained how to let go. So much of our conditional training emphasizes just the opposite—hold on, and the tighter the better! Most of our training is "mind-based" and not "heart-based." You realize the best way for you to become good at letting go is to surrender to your heart and say, "Okay, I will listen to you. I will act on what I know is right and true for me." Once your mind comprehends this, it will join *with* you instead of fighting *against* you.

In your awakening journey, you often find yourself on the "fast track." In your desire to move forward, you are literally propelled into the new, leaving the old behind. You "ride the wave the way it's going" and you do so with thanksgiving in your heart.

A Sufi saying advises, "When the heart weeps for what it has lost, the spirit laughs for what it has found." You reflect back on your life and see where this has applied. What appeared as a great loss turned into your greatest gift.

4. BUILDING TRUST

When you can see the gifts in your new life, when you can appreciate the rewards of "letting go and letting God," then you deepen your trust of life and of yourself. You move forward with greater confidence, knowing that all is right. You realize that all of life is *for you*, no matter how it looks in the moment.

This trust spreads out to all of life. You see that all of life is perfect, no matter what the "outside package" looks like. And in your building of trust, you feel more connected with life and its divine intelligence. You realize you don't have to know everything and be in control at every moment. You realize there is nothing to control. There is only who you are in each moment. There is only God pulsating through you and throughout all of life. There is only love that fuels all of you.

5. SURRENDERING ALL NOTIONS OF SMALLNESS

You are building your foundation of trust and are embracing the Christ Heart. You soon realize in order for you to fully shine, you must be willing to let go of any and all thoughts of limitation and smallness. This is yet another level of letting go which we described earlier.

You know deep within your Being the power of your thoughts, and you use your greater will to see the God in everything, especially within yourself. You don't fake it, you don't pretend that you see this when you don't. You *look* for it. You look for the God in everyone and in all of your life experiences.

You are honest with yourself about this, and you gradually feel your perception changing. In your total acceptance of yourself, a new sight opens. You see that you are gradually leaving behind any and all notions of smallness and limitation. You begin to more directly experience your vastness and connection to all of life. Your mind is open to it and this happens because you are allowing God to show itself to you. In your willingness to be open, you trade an old way of understanding for a new one.

6. LEARNING THE LANGUAGE OF ENERGY

In your expanding perception of yourself, you find all of your intuitive senses are becoming activated. These include: your clairvoyance (your inner vision), your clairaudience (your inner hearing) and your clairsentience (your inner knowing). You find yourself being more telepathic and energy sensitive. You feel and know things about yourself, others and the world around you of which you had previously been unaware, as though you are suddenly multilingual after only speaking one language.

Developing your inner senses opens you up to worlds previously unknown. You realize energy is information. As you become more fluent in the language of energy, you become more versatile in your ability to perceive and *translate* any given situation. In this ability, you are opened up to the Universe *because this is the Universal language*.

7. EXPERIENCING THE POWER OF YOUR CHRIST HEART LOVE

As you open more and more to the Christ seed within, it manifests to greater and greater degrees. This is what self-realization is all about—realizing who you truly are *already*. You have been willing to shed the old coats of ignorance and illusion so that this truth could emerge. Now you are feeling your love rising and expanding in you—nourishing, healing and enlivening you. You also witness it pouring forth as it acknowledges its "connectedness" with all living things.

You cannot help it—it simply happens. Suddenly, in the middle of the most ordinary places, you look around and realize you are feeling love for everyone! You don't even know them, but a deep recognition unveils itself, and you send your love forth to touch them. Through your direct experience of your growing love and compassion, through witnessing for yourself the results of drinking it into your psyche and sharing it with others, you are walking it, breathing it, talking it, dreaming it, eating it, loving it, living it. This is the reality of it settling into place in your daily life.

In your Christ Heart, you know your connection with God and all living things. You have opened to the universal flow of this energy that abounds everywhere. You are *in* the flow of this energy and you receive it fully. You know this is your ultimate healer. This is the energy that heals all and everything. Your gratitude for this love, this "Christedness," is immeasurable.

In your embrace of the Christ flow, you find your inner well is full of God's love, the only true love there is. Not only is your well full, but it is abundant, over-flowing to all of life everywhere. You find yourself naturally reaching out to everyone you encounter with a love, a gentleness and a kindness that touches them to their core. Your love is limitless. You have embraced the loving power of your Christ Heart.

8. NETWORK OF SUPPORT

You are experiencing the power of your Christ love and you realize you are part of the family of humanity here on Earth. You feel your connection with others, and you are now attracting those of like mind and like heart. In doing so you are surrounded by your true spiritual family of brothers and sisters. You all speak the same language and you come to this family as equals, offering each other love and support when needed, to face the challenges of your lives.

You think to yourself, "This is what life here is supposed to be about—being with and connecting with my soul family members." Your joy is overflowing with the knowledge that you are part of this beautiful band of Christ-Hearted, connected human Beings. You are grateful for the friendship and the support they offer and you value the importance of this level of family.

9. POWER AND PERSECUTION

You are now sharing your love. This is your God-power. It is the only true power that exists. All other kinds of power are false in the face of your love, your God-power.

However, in sharing your ever-flowing love, you encounter your soul memories of persecution. We have all had incarnations in which we spoke out and displayed our light, and it wasn't well received. We've all been persecuted for it in a variety of ways.

Because of these past experiences and their impact upon you at a cellular level, you might feel that you are not safe here, that you will be persecuted again this time. Your cellular memory makes no distinction between then and now—to it, the past and the present are the same. Therefore, the message it sends you is that you are in possible danger here, that you need to protect yourself at all costs, that you need to hold your divinity back.

At this step in your journey, you become conscious of the ways you have tried to hold your power back without even realizing it. One of the most exhausting things you have done is to suppress this—your beauty, your God-ness, your life force. You understand now that in doing so, you have been suffering a kind of "soul sickness" of blocked power and passion. Now you can see and feel how the pain of this has permeated your life, disturbed and distressed your body, mind, emotion and spirit.

With the strength of your emerging love and clarity, you under-stand all these things. You realize this is a critical stage of clearing in your journey. You want to heal yourself. Without clearing the persecution memories that you have associated with expressing your divine power, you know you simply cannot move forward fully. Moving forward without this clearing is like driving your car with the emergency brake on. You are able to move, but your true power is severely compromised.

Throughout this book, we speak of Jesus and the pattern of persecution. It's in all of us, and it will rear its head when we start to come out as lightworkers. Interference tends to come in strongly on the persecution vibration because, with persecution, one fears for his or her survival. You are not daunted by this. You realize it is yet another step or stage that you need to move through so that you can free yourself. As with the other steps, you know you can do it with grace, embracing each moment, or you can kick and scream all the way. You know it is simply your choice—and you choose to do it gracefully and with gratitude singing in your heart.

10. EMBRACING YOUR MULTI-DIMENSIONALITY

You have cleared your memories of persecution and now you are fully the conduit of the Christ energy. Your heart is now the Christ Heart. You both receive and give effortlessly. It is not even something you think about—it is simply your natural flow, simply who you are.

You have awakened, and life suddenly is magical! Magic is in air—sometimes in the smallest of ways and other times, it is tre-mendous! In discovering the magic of life, your joy bubbles forth. Your heart is full with connection and love, and you are bringing joy to all of life everywhere.

You have claimed your true power, the Christ Heart, and you have discovered the magic of life in all that you do. Your life is an exhilarat-ing and heightening experience. You are realizing there are many, many worlds beyond your three-dimensional construct. You are realizing that, as humans, we are not alone but are connected with a multitude of levels of consciousness and their respective energies.

You might refer to many of these energies as guides, teachers, brothers and sisters in spirit, masters, angels, nature spirits or just simply your spiritual friends. You realize it is not important what you call them, but how you interact with them. They are not here to parent you, as you are not their child. You are in conscious relationship with them because you have evolved to the point where you can co-create with them.

These Beings or energies are merely reflections of yourself. In them, you see the higher aspects of yourself. Through them, you are able to embrace those parts of yourself you might have missed without their guidance. This helps you to discover your "bigness."

Embracing yourself as a multi-dimensional Being expands the breadth of your own divine power and gives you access to vastly greater resources. It takes you beyond this world to the knowing that Earth is one of a group of planets that are being "lit up" at this time. You are no longer limited to Earth. You now experience yourself as a cosmic being with cosmic knowing, understanding, intelligence and insight. You are no longer caged in and limited to the old Earth structure of identity, movement, motion, and its rigid rules and regulations.

You are inspired to open new windows of understanding, integrity, wisdom, magic, insight, love and compassion. You suddenly find yourself free to soar in a much broader field of existence than you have yet given yourself permission to explore.

You say to yourself, "Sure, I have thought of myself as a cosmic being from time to time. I have even entertained the idea. But then, when I found myself in the grocery store identifying myself as tight, small and limited only to the human domain, I lost it. But now that is not the case! I have now redefined what it means to be human. I realize it is not Earth that has been so limited, but me and how I have defined myself on Earth."

Your new definition of being human refers to your divinity, your freedom to soar the universe and the cosmos unfettered and fully alive. That divinity talks to the Christ Heart—open and able to access wisdom from other higher levels of intelligence. Your daily life is altered because you have just altered your perception of yourself and the reality you live in. You realize you can expand your focus in a heartbeat. Wherever you place your attention, your energy will follow. If it looks a certain way on the surface then you look deeper and find that it is altogether different.

You realize being human means that you are God-Man/Woman. In your co-creation, you are setting the world on fire with light. This has been your desire all along and now you are activated to do so.

11. INTEGRATING YOUR CHRIST HEART

This step is one which courses throughout your journey. You expand and then you integrate. If you never integrate, you never have the ground upon which to move forward *fully*.

Integration takes place easily and gracefully when you adopt the attitude of *allowing*. In allowing, your energy flows and everything within you can settle and reorganize much more easily. You breath in and out with the attitude of allowing integration. You want to be grounded here on Earth because this is where you are.

The purpose of your Christ Heart is only fulfilled when it is integrated in your life. It is not just a pinnacle experience that is meant to stay in some special place inside of you. It is not enough to know about it within and not bring it forth. It continually demands that you bring your God-ness to bear in every single area of your life, thus making it your conscious breath and body.

You came here with a strong purpose and desire to bring forth your own unique gifts. You came here to experience your Mastery within this three-dimensional construct. Integrating your power is necessary in order for it to be effective here. Once integrated, you have a strong, stable and steady platform from which to express your Mastery with impact and success.

12. LIVING YOUR MASTERY

You are now living your union with God. Every thought, every action and every reaction is "impulsed" by this divine energy. You are feeling the fullness of your own well. You are flourishing in your wholeness and spreading this around the globe with intention and purpose that is inspired by joy and freedom for all. This is your power.

You are one of the "Gentle Giants." The Messiah within you is brimming with love and deep, deep compassion. You understand the needs, the aches and the pains of mankind. You understand well the agony of concealing your light. You have relinquished your own concealment and risen up through the dross like a flower breaking through the ground in the spring. You are beautiful and strong, eager to express your joy, your passion. You have seeded yourself, and now you are enjoying your beauty, your vibrancy, your color, your fragrance. You are solely focused on opening and sharing your exquisiteness so that all of life can benefit. When you have expressed the fullness of your beauty, you will pass from here and reunite with your Creator until your next sojourn.

You join hands with your brothers and sisters and with all of life everywhere. You gracefully project your love forward to embrace the energy of all future children and their children after them. You are well aware that everything you plant is purposefully done in the name of fostering love and sovereignty for all humanity, now and yet to come. Where you walk today, tomorrow all children will feel the energy of your love on the soles of their feet.

You are a leader of the new way.

You have returned to your Maker and all is well.

You go to bed each night with a smile of gratitude because you have lived another day of peace, creativity and oneness. Until the morrow, you sleep to recharge the intelligent body. You give it its due rest so that it will carry you gracefully through another day of being God in action.

You wake up on the morrow and are stirred again by your radiant joy and excitement about living. You are *awake!* You know it, and the world knows it, too. Hallelujah!

Chapter Eleven

The Earth Speaks

The Earth plays an essential role in grounding our spirits during our awakening journey. We cannot emphasize enough the importance of developing and maintaining a conscious relationship with her. This is not only important for our general sense of well-being, but also for our spiritual integration.

Both of us have always felt a very close kinship with the Earth and have always turned to her for refreshment and restoration. We have chosen to live in areas that are remote and secluded so we could be ensconced in her energy. She has been a vital part of our balance and wholeness.

Just as all of us can move into those higher aspects of ourselves for guidance, we can do the same with the Earth. Over the years, we have developed our sensitivity to her through deliberate study and inner reflection. We have actively opened the lines of communication with her different intelligences who have taught and inspired us greatly. Our experience has shown us the wealth of support, joy, wisdom and guidance that is available to us all.

We have also seen the importance of teaching others about the Earth—opening them to the wealth of possibilities of deep and abiding friendship, love, communication and inspiration with her. This has always been a most sacred part of our teaching.

We all *need* the Earth. Ignoring this vital relationship is ignoring the ground that we walk upon. *We are connected.* Whenever we are in her natural element for any length of time, we let down our guard and open up. She soothes us and restores us to our simplicity and divine natures. She cleanses us of turmoil, emotional and psychic buildup, and brings us back to clarity about ourselves and our lives. Her spirit reminds us of our own. Her spirit charges ours. To deliberately invite her into our hearts opens us to a powerful field of strength, clarity and caring. To open to her various intelligences sheds new light on vast frontiers that we yearn and need to know about. It brings us joy and profound peace.

In our awakening journey, once we are well into our expansion and into the stage of crystallizing our connection with our Christ Consciousness, the Earth enters the picture in a dynamically activated way. With her help we are able to ground our energy and cement the connection of our spirit into our physical realm. From here, our Christ Consciousness can now express in a steady, solid and grounded way.

When we invited the Earth to speak with us, she gave the following message:

"I see, feel and know that you are reaching for yourselves, to bring inside of you your own Christ crystal, to merge it into your bodies, ignite it and express the radiance of it fully through this physical plane. You have worked diligently to bring this forth, and you are well on your way to realizing your intent.

"I am here now to tell you, unequivocally, that you cannot and will not be able to do this without me. You will not be able to fully ground your spiritual consciousness into your body without me.

"So many of you think that your spiritual expression has only to do with that which is penetrating your crown and pouring through you. This is only half of it. I carry the other half of your Christ seed; I have been holding it in my belly since Jesus walked upon me and planted it there. I am the other half of the grid which will pull in and stabilize the matrix of the Christ Consciousness here now.

"I am 'physicalized' light energy, the substance through which you will be able to ground the strength and power of your spirit into this physical plane, into yourselves, into your lives, into this world.

"I am here for you. I am your shelter, I am your haven, I am your nourishment, I am your ally. I am all of these, and so much more! Many of you have opened to me more and more over the past decades. Fascinated by my energy you have come to learn about me and, through this, yourselves. This has been vitally important. Many of you have recognized the deep comfort I can bring by cleansing and clearing you from the dross of fear and chaotic energies accumulated by living in your modern times, especially in your over-populated, concrete places. You have need of me in many ways, and always will.

"When you spend time with me, you know well how I restore you to your spirit and put you and your lives in proper perspectives of simplicity, Godliness and connection. You have learned that I am an intelligence that can teach you, guide you and support you, and inspire you to great heights. You have learned that you can rely upon me. You can trust me.

"For most of you, this opening and building of trust over the past years has been a deliberate paving of the way for you to understand more fully my role now; to understand yet another dimension of my ability and purpose in your conscious lives.

"We have an agreement, you and I. We sealed it before you came here. This agreement was that I would be your ground, I would be the receiver of your light when you awoke to its power and possibilities. I would be the other end of the spectrum that would call you in from the other light dimensions and stabilize you into the light here in me. You would come into my core crystal and discover that mine is the Christ just like yours.

"Here you would find peace. Here you would find steadiness. Here you would find ground. Here you would find the ground in you.

"How do I do this, you ask. It is an awareness I speak of. It is an attitude, an understanding that opens up these lines of exchange and communication between us. Consciously bring me into your awakening process. Include me and trust me enough now to let me into you and you into me. This is not just to feel good and be soothed; it is to deliberately anchor you in so that you will *land*. You will no longer feel like an airplane circling around trying to find the airport. Once you have fully landed here, you can do whatever you want. You will be safe and strong. Your light will be here, solid as a rock—and there will no hesitation.

"Now you can bask in your spirit to your heart's content. You have grounded and cemented your realization of it *into yourself* so that you can do something with it. The more you express it, the more you realize its endless flow and divine purpose.

"I give and help you. You give and help me when you have landed and are radiating your power of love to all corners of the Earth. Then I benefit from the awakened consciousness that you have brought forward and which is touching all of humanity, directly or indirectly. You see, I need you too. We need each other in this. This is the plan.

"Let us join together now in joyous co-creation. Let us join together in loving cooperation. Let us unite together in our hearts, our minds and our bodies.

"Come to me. I am open. I am waiting. I am here and ready to receive your graciousness now. Merge with me, and we will celebrate our glorious passion together. In this way, you will have merged the radiance of your Christ crystal with mine—and the power of our light will be magnified and poured forth."

Chapter Twelve

Jesus Speaks

This chapter, devoted to Jesus and his wisdom, contains informa-tion that he expressly asked to be included in this book. As always, his messages are simple, direct, loving and profound.

Dear Ones, Good People,

You have stepped into a new horizon of your Being at this time. You have called forth your light, your wisdom and your purity of heart. It is through your love, coupled with the intelligence of your intrinsic nature, that you are now living and leading your lives. Every conscious step that you take carries the light for many to follow in your wake. As has been stated before, you do not travel alone in this incarnation—you travel with many. Together we are birthing a greater awareness of Being that is establishing a new paradigm for thousands of years to come. You are the pioneers.

We often need to look to the past to see where we have been and to decide what about it we wish to keep. Through the many steps you have taken, those that were comfortable and those that were not, you have grown strong. You have learned, you have gained your ground, you have become resilient. Through many seemingly perilous moments, you have dug deep within your hearts to find solutions, to create new attitudes, to remind yourselves that, yes, you do have what it takes to make this journey.

In those more challenging moments, you have drunk deep from your inner well, unfolding as flowers welcoming the brilliance of the sun. During the easier steps of your journey, you have been able to water your emerging strength; you have been able to nour-ish and enhance your goodness and grace. Through it all, you have found a great, deep nurturing that has spread your wings so that you now fly freely.

Every stepping stone of your pathway has enlightened you about who you are and why you are here. Each one has helped you to appreciate your vital link in this family of humankind that is now uniting in its movement forward.

Throughout this book, you have felt me guiding you through areas of yourself that needed healing. In restoring yourself to the fullness of your light, you see that I am your friend, your companion, your co-creator. But *you* are the force of God that thrusts forward. *You* initiate creation, initiate change, initiate love in the fullest sense of its Being.

I am here with you now as I have always been and always will be. Together, we can join hands as a family that includes those life forms which have seemed different or strange to you in the past, whether they be two-legged or four-legged, rooted ones, or star ones. We are all God. We are all the wholeness of the family of creation.

Be now your own peace, your own solidity, your own joy of living. Be all of this consciously, living by it day in and day out. As you move forward, take all that you have learned from your past and honor it as part of the great foundation of your Being. And from this, proceed with all the confidence and joy and desire of your Being to create *anew*. This creation is coming from your inner senses. It is coming from the fabric of your dreams. Your dreams are the vision of what is to be. They have been brought to you because they are perfect for you individually, as well as perfect for the whole. It is in realizing your dreams that you will meet your needs most appropriately, most gracefully and most effectively.

Move forward gracefully now. Be present with yourselves each moment, knowing that you are these dreams coming true. You are these dreams being made manifest. You are these dreams unfolding into the material plane. Place all of your love, all of your knowing, all of your trust in the force that moves and guides you. That force which dreamed you in the first place is the fuel that is generating this new reality. On this knowing, you can soar.

Let us walk the remaining pages together—to read, to feel, to be inspired. When we are finished, we will have yet greater clarity from which to create and deeper love to share.

Blessings to you all.

YOUR LIGHT

Feel the beating of my heart ... and how it rejoices in being joined with you. Two thousand years seems so long ago, but we both know we have been together all this time. How can there be any distance between us in the face of the love that we share? I have always been deep and close in your heart, and you have always known this. I love you.

I remember how we would walk together back then, and I would gaze into you and see in you all that I knew in myself. And I would also see that you did not recognize this in yourself—that your devotion was for me, the way I spoke and the love I lived so fully. I saw that you had not yet come into your own.

Yet I knew the moment would come when you would realize that it was not only me, Jesus, who you loved so intensely, but also yourself as God, reflected through your eyes into me and through my eyes into you. I knew that the time was coming when each one of you would realize that I was inside of you, so that my "leaving" would finally be of no discomfort. I have waited for this moment when you would truly recognize yourself—your beauty, your light, your power—as a creation of the Almighty Spirit. This is my joy both for you and for me—for you, because it signifies that you no longer need me as your guide in the old way and, for me, because it is the fulfillment of my life, my teaching, my Being. It is liberating for us both and brings us closer as friends and co-creators. You are a blessing in my life, and our loving grows ever stronger the deeper we go in ourselves.

It matters not to me how many days, years or centuries it might take in your time for any of you to discover this about yourselves or about me. It only matters to me that you matter to yourself. For those of you who are still "searching," why not realize that you have already found? As you dissolve your blindness, rejoice in the wondrousness that has always been you.

We are now joined in brotherhood and sisterhood of a different nature than we were two thousand years ago. Now you know you are mighty, your heart is filled with light and true understanding, you are the flame that burns brightly. When I look at you, I see that you see into yourself, and you witness for yourself the clarity of Christ in your own Being.

In actuality, two thousand years ago, you did not forsake yourself. I know it seemed that way, but it was not. You did not leave yourself in the dust. You were not living in my shadow; you were emerging in your own bright light. If this weren't true, you wouldn't have been able to see any light in me.

Realize that always, always, did you love yourself tenderly, then and now. You are whole, each of you. You are healed because of your own love. You do not need me or anyone to live that love for you anymore. You never did. You know that now. You are the light of your love and you always will be.

I now resign my position as your "caretaker." Your eyes are opening to the reality that I was never that in the first place. I say again, you are the light that you so loved in me. Seize this love and live it fully. We are one family of freedom, a family of love that is growing ever more magnificent! I love you—eternally.

Persecution

This subject has been addressed, yet I still have more to say about it. The subject of persecution, yours or mine, is not something that can be swept under the rug or ignored. It is critical to the essential issue—that of opening to love. Until you have cleared your idea and concept of yourselves as a victim, you cannot even begin to live your Mastery. You may think that you are, but you won't be. You will still be walking the wheel of fear. You may be living your courage, but you will doing this as a fearful person needing courage rather than as a courageous person who is loving, open and living in full trust. These are two completely different energies. Do you see and feel the difference?

As I explained when I shared my story with you earlier in the book, I was not persecuted. I understand it looked that way to everyone, but this was not so. I was not a victim, I was not helpless, I was not suffering, and I did not hold any blame or resentment toward anyone. I knew prior to that lifetime what would probably take place, and I was fully prepared and trained to handle all the events that unfolded. My dedication to my purpose and my intense and unwavering devotion to God made everything different for me than how it looked from a spectator's point of view. I had immensely strong spiritual fiber to guide me and lift me through all of my "painful" experiences. I was untouched by the pain. Rather, through these experiences, I reached untapped spiritual heights.

Remember my purpose—to seed and demonstrate living light. I was this. I did this. I am this still. With this in mind, do you understand how my own perception of what happened could be blissful and radiant? Do you understand how I could have been so loving and forgiving? Do you understand how I do not associate what happened to me with persecution?

My crucifixion was one of the most creative events of my human embodiment. Within this experience, I merged even more deeply into the seed of God. I surrendered more than I had even fathomed was possible. All the players involved in the planting of light—including my "persecutors"—played their parts beautifully. I was grateful to *all* of you.

In truth, persecution never entered into my picture. To have felt otherwise would be tantamount to my saying that someone else had power over me and my spirit. And that has never been the case. Nor has that ever been the case for you, even though you may not have recognized it.

The identity of persecution is one of self-annihilation. It is an identity of poverty and helplessness. Perceiving yourself as a victim removes from you any sense of dignity and any knowledge of your strength. That is why the identity of victimization is effective for those who want to control you. It keeps you blinded to your power. Observe also whether or not you are persecuting yourself. Often, self-persecution becomes an automatic behavior once that pattern has been set.

In truth, it is impossible to annihilate spirit, even though this may go unrecognized by those in the throes of suffering. Spirit is eternal. Spirit is mighty, always and forever.

One of the major purposes of this book is for you to have the opportunity to clear your own history of persecution and set your internal records straight. Understanding that you are far stronger than any persecution could ever be gives you a sense of your spiritual fiber. Staying attached to persecution in any way, whether through nursing an old wound or holding blame and resentment, weakens you and reduces you to fear. It sends you spinning right back onto the wheel of fear and ignorance.

When you are living fully, when you are so engaged in your purpose that your aliveness runs at full tilt, everything that you once perceived as hardship, pain, suffering and persecution looks different. In allowing the full expression of you, you have become completely spirit-identified—body, heart and soul.

Where has all the persecution gone? It is a thing of the past. Rejoice!

LOVE

So much has been said and written about love, and rightly so. Love is the "juice" that gives us all meaning in our lives.

Your true love begins with yourself and with your willingness to accept and embrace God in your heart.

You are love. It is not a state of emotion but rather your eternal state of Being. You were made of love, in love, by love. That which created you is love—therefore, you are that. Love is what makes you possible.

Be silent in yourself to reflect upon this for a while. You are deserving of that and so much more. Many of you sometimes feel love has gotten lost in your world. Many of you fear you have lost it in yourself, but this is not so. That which you are can never be lost. That which you are is always within. You may have worn many faces, many bodies, many belief systems in your travels, but there is always one constant—you, as love.

You witnessed my love for all who came before me. You experienced my love for you and were forever changed. You have witnessed your own love touching those to whom you have reached out. Deep, deep within you, you know what love is. You may think that you don't trust it. You may think that it will hurt you. But, none of this is true. These are only old feelings based on old misunderstandings. You love your love. You love to love. You love being loved. You love that you are made of love. Feel your joy about all of this.

Give up everything but love. Do this because everything but love is peripheral, divisive and illusionary. Nothing else but love matters.

Love knows no boundaries. When your heart is truly open and love is flowing through you as an exquisite extension of you, it goes beyond your own comprehension of what it is. It is divine intelligence moving from the heart of God. In its freedom, love's ability to touch, teach, heal, revitalize and inspire is unlimited.

Be free in your loving. Open your heart to all so that your love can touch everyone no matter how the "outside package" appears or acts. It's been said, "Love is the answer." I agree.

In your love, you are simple, beautiful and so very very powerful. Shine on, great love, shine on!

SINNING

Say this word ten times very fast and it will sound very silly!

Sinning is a subject which has been grossly misunderstood. The identity of "sinner" is one that has been primarily used for the purpose of manipulation for control and power. It effectively keeps your life force contained and your freedom limited. Many of you have swallowed this identity whole. You literally took it inside of you and made it part of your fabric.

Many of you perceive yourselves as "sinning agents" that need to be carefully watched and evaluated. You need to be either rewarded or punished. Most of you feel this way to varying degrees, either consciously or unconsciously.

It is time for the entire concept of behavior, good and bad, to be properly understood. There is no such thing as "sinner" in the context in which it has been placed. To sin, as defined by your dictionary, simply means "to err." It is viewed as positive information through which a learning about self and conduct can be understood. Every action is designed to teach you something. If you do not learn from your action, it repeats itself until you do.

The Law of the Universe awards no points for either "good" or "bad" behavior. It is neutral, you understand. It does not see through the eyes of judgment. Action is simply recorded. For every action, there is a reaction. Cause and effect.

In your actions, you are the activator. Through your actions, you are also the receiver of the effects. You have many phrases which explain this well: "What you put out, comes back." "What goes around comes around." "You reap what you sow." All of these are true. This is the "universal record keeping" at work. There is no punishment, no reward. There is only the flow of energy generated by your intent.

Your action, whatever it may be, will return to you at some point in your evolution. Know this. Whatever you do unto others is exactly what will be done unto you. Count on it. Act wisely. Learn from your behaviors so that you may consider their effect with understanding and grace.

Why am I speaking about this now? Because to identify yourself as a "sinner," with all the attendant judgment and guilt, is a trap. It is a trap which you perpetuate. It is time to cleanse and clear this now. It is a faulty thought pattern that you can change.

Believe in yourselves now. Support yourselves in your goodness. Move out of the fear and into the support of yourselves as loving Beings capable of loving action. Joyously take responsibility for yourselves as free agents. You do not need to bind yourselves at every turn because you are afraid of doing the wrong thing. Trust yourselves. Trust God in you. Live this.

Never be afraid if you have erred. Look closely at what the experience has brought you and use this information to clear your course. Be grateful for its teaching and wisdom. You are the better for it.

If your action has hurt someone else, do what you can to rectify the situation. If there is need for forgiveness, forgive and be forgiven. Forgiveness is the grace that transmutes all energy into a positive, life-enhancing flow. When you have completed this, move on and give no further thought to it. Look only to the gift it has brought you and use it wisely in your future.

You are not a "sinner." You never have been. You never will be. Such a thing only exists in the minds of man. It does not exist in the universe. Whether or not you keep this in your identity or whether you set yourself free remains your choice.

JOY

Joy is your birthright. It is your fundamental nature. Simply by being alive, you are joy. *Joy is God unmasked.*

The more awake you are to your beautiful, shining, exquisite Being, the more you feel your joy, know your joy and express your joy. The more fully aligned you are with your essence, the more joy you are. The more joy you are, the more joy there is because joy attracts joy! And joy begets joy.

You are all beautiful and happy Beings! You are joyous when you are riding the currents of creation and sharing yourselves with all of life everywhere. When you are letting your joy ring freely you are in pure joining with your Maker. It is pure infusion of Self.

Many of you have believed that you needed to hide your joy, not only from the world but from yourselves! Why keep this beauty such a secret? To "fit in" and appear inconspicuous? Has it worked? Do you feel better for it?

Can you laugh about it now and bring yourself out of your own dark closet?

If you do not feel your joy, or if you feel cut off from it in some way, it is because you are living just on the edge of your heart. Many of you stop yourselves from leaping into the fullness of your sacred heart because you are afraid you will lose something by doing so. You are right! You will! You will lose your suffering and disconnection. Every way you choose to live is exactly that, a choice.

Many of you think that your joy is dependant upon other people or events. This is not so. There is far too much joy in you for this to be the case. You *are* your joy. When, where and how much you wish to be it is entirely up to you. It is controlled by nothing out-side of you. It is a barometer of how connected you are with your own fountain of Being.

Your joy is a deeply running current that nurtures you as you go about your business on planet Earth. It meanders and pours it-self through the pathways of your knowing. Your mind may fre-quently think that your daily tasks are distasteful or boring. The mind is often dissatisfied with many things which the soul finds quite rewarding. Isn't it funny how this works?

Become more attuned to yourself. To what parts of yourself are you listening in your daily activities? Perhaps there is infinitely greater joy in what you are doing, being and experiencing than you have known.

Your joy is as intrinsic to you as breathing is to your physical body. Joy is not a luxury to acquire, but a treasure which you already are in infinite abundance. Embrace yourself so fully that joy is in perpetual motion through you.

Your joy is the sweet, simple song of your soul resounding through your body and through your creative momentum. It is action, it is impulse, it is movement in full alignment with your Source. Joy is yours to trust and in so doing you trust and give way to your highest impulses and most deeply connected knowing. Your joy is a great blossoming of all the brilliance of you. Sometimes it is loud, sometimes it is soft, sometimes it is a steady hum of God's bliss.

Joy, its acceptance and reverence, is the new paradigm of living for this world.

You may feel that you have come to an Earth which cannot receive your joy. This is not so. Earth herself rings out this very same joy. The stars, moon and sun pour forth this very same joy. All of you, in your core, possess this very same joy. You can reveal your joy here because there is resonance with it here. You need your joy; all of life needs your joy.

God's life is the only life there is. Everything else is just a dance around the ring of the circle, not in the center itself. Come into your center. This is the source of your joy. Your joy asks nothing of you. It does not take from you. It energizes and enriches all that you are and all that is. *Joy is God laughing you!*

You do not need to hide your exuberance for life anymore. The more you reveal, the more you will know the abundance of joy all around you.

Let your joy guide your way. Stay true to this divine nourishment. It is your fuel, it is your Truth, it is your power. Light up the Earth with the full freedom of your joy, loud and clear for all to hear. Do it for yourself. Do it because it feels so good. Only the best can ever be born out of this!

ASCENDED MASTERS AND ASCENSION

Ascended Masters are Beings that have evolved their consciousness so much that they are able to transmute and transcend matter.
We (I am one) operate within the context of the God energy, the
principles of LOVE.

We are close to you because this is our service at this time in
our own evolvement. We are with you to teach you, to inspire you
and to help you in your expansion. Our assistance is as much a
contribution to our own growth as it is to yours. Know this. This is
important.

Many individuals upon your plane have difficulty with the
notion of Ascended Masters. Even within the context of your New
Age, there are many who scoff at and scorn the idea of these Beings.
This is due mostly to misunderstanding and misinterpretation.

We have often been spoken of in ways that are very "airy-fairy,"
ungrounded and fantastical. Unfortunately, these notions misrep-
resent the truth of who we really are. In fact, we are very solidly
grounded in our understanding of, and relationship to, your physical world. It is because of our substantial working knowledge and
expertise about living light on planet Earth that we can even be of
service to you.

The whole subject of Ascension has become very popular over
the years and has also taken on some very confusing connotations.
For some, it is seen as an escape and a means of not dealing with
physical reality. None of this is what it is really all about. At this
time, I wish to clarify.

Ascension is the shift from the "mortal mind" way of living to
a much broader and all-encompassing "immortal mind" perspective. One conveys limitation; the other conveys freedom. It is the
Ascension from the mortal point of view to the immortal one. It is
the *attunement* to, and *embodiment* of, this understanding.

Ascension is the experience of transmuting matter and mortal-
ity wherein the frequency is so refined that it can *include* matter
but is not dominated by it. The individual who has reached this
state of evolved consciousness is free to choose in what matter to

be and when to be in it. Matter becomes something over which this individual has dominion rather than the other way around.

By its very nature, you can see that Ascension is a very evolved state. It is a pathway open to all of you who wish to devote your energy and effort in this direction. It is a path of freedom.

Give yourselves permission to walk your path of Ascension, as well as to welcome those of us who serve you as exemplary role models. By being open to receive us, you will have opportunities to move very quickly and grow with delight. Please note, we Masters are *not* to be placed above you and be therefore unreachable by you. This would serve nothing except to perpetuate the framework of separation which is exactly what we are all endeavoring to diffuse.

Expanding and refining your consciousness asks that you make changes in how you see things. You have the choice of seeing your pathway as a struggle, as a difficulty, as a relentless obstacle course. Or you can view it as a journey of freedom wherein you are flexible, resourceful, spontaneous and endlessly creative. You can be in constant conflict with yourself or you can let go and graciously receive the simple blessing of you.

As you mature spiritually and feel comfortable in yourselves, you will find that your emphasis upon life and its variety of faces changes. You will become less serious about the significance of each single flicker of change and more appreciative of simply an endless flow of the "universal flowering."

Each of these choices reflects in which mind set you are moving at any moment—the mortal or immortal. Remember, you can re-choose at any second. You are bound by nothing except that which you have created for yourself in each moment.

Remember that love is your foundation. It is this you are learning. It is this you are embracing as your consciousness moves from mortal to immortal. Love is the nourishment of your Being which liberates you.

Choose to trust your own love and act on this choice. This is when the moment of Ascension begins.

We wish you a happy journey of being masterful as the moments pass.

CONDITIONING

As you have been told many, many times, and will be told again, your conditioning is like a giant wrapping which enfolds your true Being. It changes and moves from incarnation to incarnation depending upon the state and status of the moral, social and cultural fiber into which you choose to be born.

Your conditioning is there to give you a structure or framework through which to relate to the particular position you have entered. It is not there to govern your life, but rather to help you in adapting yourself to the moment and morality of the time. It gives you a complete education as to what exists and what is expected by those around you. This is *only* information. It is not designed to script your destiny unless you yourself give it the power to do so. Your conditioning, once you have matured enough to recognize it for what it is, becomes supremely malleable and offers itself to you as a substance which you can then mold according to the true desires of your soul. The choice of self-government is then yours. It is as fluid as you understand it to be. This is the aspect of free will inherent within all systems of life.

Never think that your conditioning is recorded in stone. It is not, unless you make it so. Recognize that there is something else that is vastly more tangible to you, more fragrant to you, more familiar to you, more understanding of you, more supportive of you, more aware of you, more loving of you, more significant to you. It is your essence, your light, your soul which is far, far greater in both substance and influence than any amount of conditioning could ever be. In as much as you have free will, however, you are free to be guided by the path you choose.

If you choose your conditioning, then so be it. If you choose your soul, then at that moment of your choosing, your conditioning becomes as the mist of illusion fading away with the dust of time.

FORGIVENESS

Forgiveness is one of the sweetest sounds you will ever hear. It is the sound of God flowing freely and joyously again.

How challenging it must be for you to live in a "stop and start" world! How uncomfortable it must be to control the very fluid of your Being as you decide who deserves rewards and who deserves punishment. How uncomfortable it must be inside of you as you grate up against your own rigid laws, rules and expectations of behavior.

It is against the fluidity of your nature to be so controlling. It is counter to your life-force when you decide how and when to punish yourself.

Forgiveness is freedom. It costs nothing and asks no more of you than your willingness to let God rule the world, inside and out. *You* do not need to keep a scorecard of all the events and people that you think are less than acceptable. *You* do not need to hold resentment because someone didn't know any better. And *you* do not need to be the unrelenting taskmaster who bears little or no loving or understanding toward yourself.

Many of you have hardened your hearts. This does not bode well for those of you who are so light-filled and longing for freedom. In order to be free, you *must* learn the art of forgiveness. Learn it now. Learn it well. It is restoring yourself to the fluid nature of your loving and Being.

When you do not forgive, you cast yourself as a victim. When you blame, you have given your power to another; you have given your precious life fluid away. When you hold resentment, you have closed the door to your heart. This can make you very sick. It can eat you up inside. All of these attitudes are alien to your nature.

You watched me be forgiveness in action. I could have chosen to be bitter and angry, to judge what happened as unfair and cruel. In judging this way, would I ever have been able to rise in love and liberation? No! I would have been trapped in the great pit of pain and injustice; I would have been imprisoned by a belief that others had power over me and my spirit.

No. I would not let this be so because I knew differently. I knew that every player was there to support what I was doing. I was grateful to them. I was grateful to you.

Most things in your lives are bigger than your ability to grasp on the purely emotional, mental human level. You must reach for the wisdom of your spirit to understand so much of what takes place for you personally and in your world around you. Do this and you will gain great insight into the gifts that are being directed your way.

Trust yourselves. Trust life. Open your heart and keep it open wide. This will keep you eternally engaged with your loving, your clarity, your strength, your compassion and your understanding. Be witness to this great power unfolding in you as you reach always for the highest that you are.

Forgiveness is your great joy—your wealth of love makes it so easy. It will restore you to your rightful power and free up your energy so that you can soar magnificently. Behold yourselves! You are brilliant!

Forgive. It is so much easier than holding back your life force. Forgive generously. God will take care of the rest.

This is your love in action.

Worthiness

Let worthiness no longer be a question in your thoughts. Know that if such a question exists at all, it is *ONLY* within the realms of your conditioned mind. Therefore, it is false. Therefore, it is illusion. Do not spend one more minute of your precious life force agonizing over whether or not you are worthy. Release yourself to your glory.

Behold yourself as God.
Value yourself.
You are valuable.

Did I Die for Your Sins?

Of course I did not die for your sins. To state that I would die for your sins is to place you below me. It is to eradicate your very own knowing that *you* are God. To say that I died for your sins is to annihilate you. It is to take away your magnificence and leave you feeling barren of passion.

There are many who do not understand what I say here, but the truth of the matter is that, two thousand years ago and today, my view is no different.

You and I are equals. It is true that I have developed my insight, my clarity, my knowing, my peace, my conscious Mastery more than you have. And it is for this reason that I can be as a guide to you in these areas. It is because I comprehend and know fully the greatness that I truly am. It is because I know that my source is universal greatness itself.

In my travels with you two thousand years ago, I conveyed to you that you were greatness as well. Why would I then be hanging on the cross saying to you that I was dying for your sins when this very attitude would mean that I understood you to be inferior and less than me? It is not in keeping with who I am to hold this philosophy.

Your radiance is bright, it is bold, it is magnificent. It always was. Take it. Own it. Claim it now. Pull off the shroud of guilt that has held you bound in poverty of spirit, isolation and great trembling all this time.

I am not here to perpetuate pain. I am here to release the knowledge that all men and women are free, that all Beings are free, that all of life is free. It was created thus, and will be thus through eternity.

This is my message. This is my love to you.

Thank you for giving me this opportunity to speak on this subject.

CHRIST CONSCIOUSNESS

Many of you speak often of "Christ Consciousness" and yet, for most of you, this remains a mystery in your understanding. As long as your perception of Christ Consciousness is that it is simply an amorphous concept swimming outside of you, you will feel cut off from yourself. It is time to change this. It is time for you to re-integrate yourself fully as the Christ that you are. It is time for you to own and live the true power of your sacredness. Let me define it here clearly and, as I speak about it, you will feel it vibrating deeply within you.

The word "Christ" refers to your Divinity. This is the sacred substance of which you are made. It is the sacred seed and essence of God that you are. It is you as purity, as innocence, as truth, as love. Understand clearly that your Christedness is not something that you *attain*. It is the very essence, the very substance that *you already are*. You are the child of your magnificent and adoring Source, therefore you are that precious and powerful substance also.

The term "Christ Heart" is used in this book in reference to the divine heart within you that knows that you are always in the heart of God and that you *are* the very heart of God. Typically, people associate loving with the heart, and your Christ Heart refers specifically to your ability to love and live from your divinely inspired point of view. Through the passion of your Christ Heart, you reach forth freely as God, as love. You perceive the world, the events around you and all of your own experiences through your expanded sense of knowing and understanding.

The term "Christ Consciousness" refers to you being *conscious* that you are Christ. It is you being fully conscious on all levels of your awareness that you are God, that you are Divine. It is you embodying this, it is you taking responsibility for this, it is you adoring and enjoying yourself as this.

To summarize this very clearly, your Christ Consciousness is your *awareness* (consciousness) that you are *divine* (Christ). Living your Christ Consciousness is *living your divinity.* It is letting this be the governing energy of your life in every way, on every level. It means that your thoughts, your attitudes, your actions and all that springs forth from you is the direct expression of the principles of truth, love and integrity that are inherent within your divine nature. These are the principles you live by.

If you are truly living this state of consciousness, you stand out amongst the masses because of the undeniable peace, glow and glory that emanates from your eyes, heart, words and movement. This presence which speaks of your centeredness and knowing that you are the love and life of sacredness expressing here and now, touches everyone and everything around you. It is what you witnessed emanating from me. It is what you so loved in me. Now you must love it so deeply in yourself that you bring it fully to life.

As you embody this reality, you change your life. You change how you think, how you feel, how you breathe, how you imagine, how you behave, how you create, how you respond, how you teach, how you touch, how you share. It alters every cell in your body to vibrate in harmony with your true joy for life.

Being actively conscious of yourself as sacred and divine in a world where people typically view themselves as being completely cut off from their Source of all life, sets you apart. Living the divine principles of your Christ Heart means you act differently as well. This also sets you apart. Is this something that scares you? Or does it tickle you? If it scares you then you are still perceiving yourself as separate from your Christedness. If it tickles your fancy then you are well ensconced in it.

Be willing to be different. After all, you've always felt that way anyway, haven't you? If you feel like you are standing alone, be proud of it. The more you honor your sacred wisdom and live by it, the more you will feel part of the "larger family" and the more you will understand the "bigger picture".

Look inside of you to receive your Christ Consciousness now. Bring it forth from within so that you are aware of how integrated in this you already are and *have always been*. Be now as the fountain of this knowing. This will cement your power as the light, love and joy of God.

Resurrect yourselves.

You are Christ. CONSCIOUSLY BE CHRIST NOW.

RESURRECTION VS. CRUCIFIXION

To Crucify: to torture, to agonize, to persecute, to execute.

To Resurrect: to restore, to come back to life again, to rise from the dead.

Which state of Being do you prefer?

How would your lives be if there were no crosses to bear? This is a state of mind which is worthy of investigation.

Liberation. Freedom. Only you can bring these to yourself.

Living, whether in a body or beyond one, is a continual state of fluidity which is governed largely by the attitudes which you hold. Your belief systems about how and who you are can be altered in the blink of an eye.

How do you think your world would be if it was my resurrection which dictated how people viewed me instead of me hanging there, bleeding on a piece of wood? What would be different about the whole picture if it was dominated by the infusion of inspiration governing the action of resurrection? How would things be if the foundation was one of living by all the principles of *that* event in my history?

I am not asking these questions to explore organized religion. I am asking them to explore *you*. How would you be if you placed all your emphasis upon yourself as a liberated, joyous, masterful, transcendent Being, and no emphasis upon yourself as a suffering sinner? Crucifixion or resurrection—through which lens do you view yourself? Which one dominates how you treat yourself?

My crucifixion and my resurrection marked two of the most creative experiences I had in that incarnation. They were both vortices of light, and yet only one was selected to be the major signpost upon which the primary foundation of Christian consciousness has been built over the past two thousand years.

I am making an observation, here, which is worthy of your consideration. Think about the foundation that has ruled your life. Think about it clearly and decide for yourself if this is the ground you wish to have under your Being. What changes do you wish to make in this now?

What happens to the picture of *YOU* if you substitute my resurrection for all the pieces that have held my crucifixion? Think of yourself as a jigsaw puzzle that is being redesigned. When you are put all together in your new design, what do you see? Who are you now? You have a choice.

THE CROSS

What comes into your mind when you think of a cross? Do you suddenly feel pain, suffering, guilt, and heaviness? Is the symbol of the cross beautiful or disturbing to you? What does it mean to you, if anything?

Just as the misunderstandings about my life have needed to be cleansed, so the energy of the symbol of the cross is asking to be cleansed.

Within your physical body, you will become increasingly aware of a power point just above the region associated with your heart center where your intimate awareness of your oneness with the cosmos and your oneness with the Earth meet. At this meeting point, the power of this love is propelled outward to either side and you discover that you are, in fact, vibrating radiantly in the shape and color of a golden cross. Perhaps you will appreciate the irony in realizing that this shape of the cross is truly a blessed and God-powered symbol of pure joy, love and creative passion.

As you feel the glory and ecstatic energy of this pulsating light within your own body, you will heal your association with this symbol that has long represented only pain and persecution for so many. In this way, yet another piece of the ancient puzzle is resurrected and transformed.

From now on, be open to honoring the light of the cross as a symbol of freedom, fulfillment and triumph of spirit.

SUFFERING

Suffering? You don't need to suffer! You have never needed to suffer but you didn't know this. You thought that this was a holy and noble thing, not to mention that it has been the conditioning of your lives many times over.

I did not suffer. Not once did I suffer in my lifetime. You may have thought I did, but I knew better than to suffer. My spirit was far too free to consider suffering as a valid way of experiencing anything.

If you are suffering, change this. If your circumstances or attitudes are causing you to suffer, change them. If your belief systems are causing you to suffer, change them. If your behaviors are causing you to suffer, change them. You have much greater control over your life than you have ever opted to accept. Now that you are merging with your spirit, you will realize that you, spirit-united, have total control.

Ask your spirit for guidance and direction in these changes you wish to make. Look around your life and examine yourself carefully so that you can pinpoint those areas that are causing you to suffocate yourself and diminish your light. Ask that the enormous power of your spirit come forth and pave the way for new ground upon which you can walk. Let your spirit do the talking and the walking. Be a positive and trusting student of your spirit. Be guided by the very greatness of your Being. Take positive action on your own behalf.

It is not in your nature to suffer. It is counter to your life force and only inhibits and denies the power and joy of your light. What could possibly be natural about this? In choosing to suffer, you are perpetuating victimization. Rise up! Take charge of the truth that there is another, more effective way of living. Take charge of your own happiness and fulfillment. Your fulfillment is entirely up to you.

You are creating new patterns now. The old ones that have been passed down through generations are being diffused and dissolved. What is replacing them? Your joy! Your freedom! Your constructive creativity! Your absolute delight in being alive here on Earth!

Be assertive in establishing your new patterns. Do this with confidence and strength. Plant yourself the way *you* want to be.

Create your life the way *you* know and desire it to be. Fulfill yourself. Fulfill the God in you. Fill your life to overflowing with the full radiance of your joy and zeal.

Suffering? Out the window! You have moved out of the land of suffering into the land of joy. *This* is your true nature. Own it!

DEATH

I see that so many of you still hold fear about death. This is your own fear and it is also the fear state held by the collective unconscious that resides in the ethers of your planet. You could say that this fear "comes with the territory." As you embody more and more of your resonant light and you are lifted up in your understanding of the mechanics of life in the three-dimensional plane, your view of death also shifts accordingly.

Let us take this time now to reevaluate what this means to you. Know that death, unto itself, is not an agent of pain, nor of hurt, nor of anguish for the one dying. Death brings sadness only to those left behind. And, this too, is predominantly because of the misunderstanding and confusion surrounding this inevitability.

Those who have lived fully will tell you they do not fear death. They are not afraid to leave something which has so enriched them, in which they have fully participated and with which they now feel satisfied and complete. They are at peace with it. This does not mean that they may not wish to extend their time on Earth for one reason or another, but the actuality of death itself does not frighten them. Usually, it is those who have not begun to live yet that fear death the most.

Death is a state of life. It does not matter whether you have your present body or another one, whether you are on this three-dimensional plane or another one, your life continues no matter what happens. Your consciousness continues to grow and keeps moving in your purpose of expressing greater and greater freedom, greater and greater aliveness. The passing, called death, is a remarkable entry into a state of peace and contentment of spirit. It is a rebirth of the most beautiful and sacred nature. It is nothing to fear; it is but another of life's transitions to be greeted fully with alertness and gratitude. Meet it being awake—that is the greatest experience of all.

Look into your own heart and see for yourself what you understand about death which has perhaps haunted you in one way or another during your Earthwalk. You do not know exactly how you will greet this great friend, Death, until the moment comes. For now, it is yours to hold in a position of grace, just like any other sacred traveling companion. In doing this, the sweetness of it comes to teach you and helps you even further to live in the moment and derive the greatest abundance from this action of living called your Earthwalk. There is purpose to every season. Why would your departure from here be any different?

Embrace your wisdom and your oneness in understanding death, and you will free yourself from that which has bound you. Make death your companion who will come when that moment is ripe for you to fall off this particular tree, when you are ready to be the sustaining nourishment for your next sojourn in the universe. Then you will be at peace and more alive here than ever before. Know this. Take care of this matter now.

Nature

Do you remember during our wandering from town to town, when at night we would sleep under the stars and be grateful for yet another day of living and loving? Do you remember when I would speak of our oneness with nature, with all aspects of it? Do you remember how much I loved this Earth?

One of the most glaring discrepancies in your modern times is your increasing separation from nature. You are removing yourselves from the very support that you so need and desire. Maintaining yourselves in your four-walled existences keeps you, in most cases, much too removed from your natural world. And by maintaining your distance from nature, you remain distant from yourselves.

Removing yourselves from the very support that is inherently so necessary and vital to your well-being as humans will undeniably have a major impact. It is like having a foundation in your house that is not properly rooted in the ground. This would obviously make your house unstable. So it is with all of you. So much of what troubles you in your modern world stems from your separation from nature.

I cannot emphasize enough the importance of you, in your own way, finding your way back to nature. Otherwise your spirit will never be able to fully ground itself into your body here in this incarnation. I implore you to *feel* what it is like to have your bare feet on the earth, to get your hands dirty in the earth, to lie unencumbered with your back on the earth, to look up at night and see the stars shining above, to wake up to the sounds of the birds beckoning to you, to feel grateful for the warmth of the sun upon your face, to be refreshed by the cleansing rain.

Nature is what enables you to put things into their proper perspective. It is the ground that you so need. Make it your priority to get back to it. Strive to stretch yourselves beyond your limitations of how you can be in nature. Spend as much time as you can there and then spend more. Live in a "primitive" setting for a while and see how this will enable you to fully come into YOUR true nature.

Make this important in your life. It is!

Peace

When you trust, you find your inner peace. In trusting, there is no question, no condition, no confinement. There is only acceptance, listening and gratitude for what is.

You experience peace when you have merged your mind with your heart. In your heart lies your peace. In your heart lies your trust.

You are peace when you are one with God.

Peace is always a choice. Many of you have experienced it here and there, and when you have, you have loved it. You yearn to have more of it. You can.

Make it your choice. Choose peace instead of struggle, instead of distraction, instead of taking sides, instead of limiting or confining yourself. Take yourself out of these parameters and walk gracefully into your field of wholeness and trust. It is not about suppression or denial; it is about choosing another way. It is choosing the way of serenity and grace that is always open to you. Rest there and you will know your peace.

It is this simple. It is this beautiful. You are this divine.

Shifting Frequencies

You have felt yourself and everything around you shifting. This is true. You are indeed shifting frequencies. You are shifting from a slow, dense frequency to a higher, vastly more refined frequency. In this shifting, you find that events move more quickly. You see the narrowing of the gap between thought and the manifestation of that thought.

You often sense yourself to be "out of time and space," and that your inner awareness is opening to a deeper Truth than you have ever known. Everything about you, your life and your world, is moving at a faster pace than ever before. When you look around at world events, you see great extremes of behavior being played out. It is as though everything on your planet has been magnified, and this is so.

I, and the many great ones who are with you, urge you to be excited about this. Gather your vast wealth of courage and bring it to bear in your conscious arena now. We understand that the momentum of life is faster than you have known and that your usual reaction is to feel uncomfortable and to reach out to compensate for this in one way or another. Before you react again, recognize within you an inherent ability to be highly flexible, fluid and malleable in the face of change.

Contrary to the human conditioning, change is something that really suits you and suits you well. Your emotional body may require some additional coaching on accepting and adapting to this truth in you, but if you look at the sweetness of your inner nature you will find an easy place about it all.

We are your friends. I am your friend, dear and Beloved. I am the Jesus that you always knew and have longed to know again in a more complete and whole way. Trust me when I tell you that this opening is your very own Christ seed emerging through the portals of your very own heart. This is what we shared together so long ago and what is now being reborn through your conscious spirits into the planes of Earth and all that live upon her. It is the Christ seed emerging.

Take your time to digest and absorb all that is happening within you. Be compassionate and loving of the many changes and transitions you are making. And no matter how your world is turning, never be afraid for yourself or for life. This opening is about life. This seed of truth is here to wrap its arms around you and carry you on to eternal freedom and joy. Perhaps this sounds like too tall an order for you. Perhaps you find yourself wanting to say, "Stop! Listen, Wait!"

There is no waiting, Beloved. The Earth is moving too fast and so are you. The train is already moving swiftly on its tracks. But rest easy. This is not going to take your life away, it is only going to add more life to you. It is the awakening into great freedom for which you have so longed.

Step into your grace now. Relish the exquisiteness of your own unique gifts as they express. Take heart, and take the hand of your own love which rushes so richly through you from God. Remember who you are. You are the light of God manifesting now, and it is for this that you came to Earth at this time.

Sink into what is happening. Join the parade. We are all in this together. Stand up for yourself and take your rightful place in this renaissance of light. *Be alive. Be full. Be free, right now!*

PASSION

Your passion is your creation unleashed. Your passion is the thrust of your creativity bursting joyously beyond the confines of your mind. Your passion is you beholding your beauty and placing it ahead of you as the great torch to light your way. Your passion is what creates the seed that creates the flower that creates the fragrance that creates the beauty.

So important is your passion, for it is your divine generator. It is like a great fiery furnace in you that sustains you. It is your vitality. It makes life fun, rewarding, delicious and intensely meaningful. It is rich, and you are rich in it.

Your passion is your fortitude. It gives you endurance so that you are still enthusiastic and vital long after the sun goes down. It is the give-and-take, the loving and mutually satisfying exchange of life with life. It springs from your inner knowing that all of life is here for your learning—to be honored, tasted, touched, felt, seen and shared. It is your enthusiasm boiling over!

You are passion. It is your life force. It is unlimited.

My Enjoyment

Those of you who knew me witnessed how much I thoroughly enjoyed living on Earth. I never took any moment for granted.

I treasured not only each of you and everyone whose life I touched, but I also treasured all the different demonstrations of life. I treasured the skies with their variety of expression; I treasured the waters with their different faces of fluidity; I treasured the plant kingdom, so alive and abundant; I treasured the mountains, always so strong and stable; I treasured the desert, quiet, serene and yet most alive; I treasured all the animals and creatures, the winged ones, the two-leggeds, the four-leggeds, the multi-leggeds. All of life was, and continues to be, so very precious to me. I thoroughly enjoy it all.

I know how easy it is for all of us to take things for granted until we lose what we have. My joy was rooted in my acceptance and embrace that all of life is in a state of constant change. I knew I had better enjoy it thoroughly because it was soon to become something else!

The sensuality of your planet is a wondrous thing to behold. Knowing what I knew about the different aspects of life expression in different dimensions, I was able to fully appreciate and enjoy the sensuality and the emotional aspects of Earth life. The instrument you call your body is a wondrously and spectacularly refined vehicle that enables the senses to thoroughly enjoy the Earth. Much too much of this is taken for granted by many of you.

Some of you will recall those times when our joy was so huge that we all "belly-laughed" together! Some of you will recall those times when we were totally enraptured with one another. When you think of me, please don't think of me as being solemn for *I was a most joyous Being!*

Let that thought permeate you and let it inspire you to new levels of enjoyment in yourself. I rejoice in your rejoicing!

Freedom

Freedom is truly all there is. You are already free. You are simply on the path of discovering this. Each one of you is a complete and unified God-being on your own journey of self-illumination.

Freedom is something for which many of you pray. Realize that freedom is an *internal* state of being. It is not external. It has nothing to do with externals.

For you to experience your freedom, you must be willing to dismantle the belief systems and thought patterns through which you have relinquished your freedom. You are not a victim. Nothing nor anyone outside of you is governing you—unless you so choose.

Who are you without the identity of "victim" on any level? Who are you as a free Being?

In releasing yourself from all bondage, and no longer choosing to regard and experience yourself as a victim of self, people, things, events, organizations, systems, you become your own Master. You take full responsibility for yourself as a magnificent Being of God-power. You own and understand your spiritual wealth and heritage.

In the context of freedom, you perceive the world and yourself very differently.

From this moment on, be clear in your freedom. Rejoice in it. Respond to your immense abilities and watch your joy unfold.

Freedom is your birthright. It is your soul-right. You came here to experience it. You came here to share it.

Freedom is your enlightenment.

It begins the moment you choose it.

YOUR PURITY

Your purity is your Divine Centering. It is your true nature. It is the core of your Essence. Many of you talk about being centered and knowing your essence. Many of you long for it, even pine for it. Many of you work very hard trying to become centered, thinking it is mainly about clearing the mind. That is only part of it. It is primarily about opening and clearing the heart.

Entering your purity is a Divine act of self-love in its simplest form. Feel it as I speak it to you. The vibratory frequency of your purity is the very highest vibration that you can manifest, whether that be through physical or non-physical form. It is the very highest in you. It is the very highest that you are.

Your purity is your state of true Being wherein only freedom is known, wherein only love is known, wherein only safety is known. I find it interesting that so many of you wonder if you will be safe if you enter your purity when, in fact, it is precisely *in* your purity that you will know all the safety you could ever want. In your purity the issue of safety becomes irrelevant; it has no meaning there. There are not even words for it there.

Many of you associate the word "vulnerability" with your purity. You fear that if you are so pure, you will be vulnerable to attack, to criticism, to alienation, to hurt. You believe that in being vulnerable, you are exposed and naked, too wide open in your physical world.

What you have not understood clearly is that in your purity lies your strength, lies your confidence, lies the total presence of Being. Therefore it is your seat of greatest knowledge, greatest love, greatest power, and, through all of that, greatest protection.

Your purity brings you *present*.

Your purity does not make you "vulnerable." It makes you invincible. In this state of soul-filled invincibility you are consciously *free* through every atom, molecule and resonant sound of your Being.

In living your purity, you move out of discord, separation and turbulence and into a world of peace, of passion, of the smooth and loving caress of universal spirit engaging fully through the material framework.

This is bliss in action. It can be very fiery, it can be very forceful, it can be supremely gentle, it can be inspiring. It is awesome. It is magnificent.

Your purity. Enter it, live it, abide by it. It is your key. It is your key to your own highest. It is your key to the highest in all of life everywhere. Is this not what you have been looking for? It awaits you.

YOUR POWER

You are so powerful! The power of your love, of your Light, of your passion, of your Being is so very, very strong that nothing can taint or diminish it. This has always been true and always will be.

Your power is waiting for you to claim it, know it, reveal it and express it. It is waiting for you to merge with it so that you can experience yourself as God.

So many of you have lived in fear of your power; afraid that you would be cast out or alienated because of it. This can only happen if you alienate yourself from it. You will not be persecuted for it unless you are persecuting yourself already. This has been addressed at length in this book; the connections between power and persecution have been made very clear.

I want you to know now the extent, depth, range and capacity of your power. Feel this. Stretch yourself to feel it even more. You are breathtaking and there is nothing that you cannot be or do if your desire and intent solidly support it. It is that simple.

You are an experience to behold. You are made of such strong and mighty fiber that you are, indeed, invincible. You may feel fragile at times, but you are not. Nothing about you is fragile. It is only your attitude and your understanding that need reevaluating.

Again, I say, nothing about you is fragile. You are a strong and mighty tower of Light, beaming and reverberating all across this planet and through the universe beyond. I am moved by you. We are all moved by you. The deeper you move into yourself, the more you will know the truth of your glorious and sacred power.

Face yourself now. Invite yourself into your world of conscious power. Touch your inner wisdom that guides it and the God that you are that fuels it. Make new decisions about who you are based on the truth that is now revealing itself to you. Act according to these truths with all of your passion and excitement for living.

Your power is potent. Set it free! Let it thrust, let it soar, let it glide, let it caress, let it be as a giant flame of love burning exuberantly in this world. As you do this, all parts of you will heal in the face of this loving fluid now flowing freely.

GRACE

This is one of the attributes that many of you identify so strongly with me. You witnessed my grace with you and everyone with whom I came into contact. You witnessed my grace with all of life.

Why was I so graceful? Quite simply because I was in Union with my Father. The peace that surpasses all understanding was mine. I was at peace. I was in peace. I was in Union.

In my grace, I glided through my days and nights in complete knowing that all was perfect. I flowed easily. My trust brought me peace. There was no struggle, only loving acceptance.

Grace lives within each of us and flows outward to all of life. You have the same ease inside of you. Now is the time to call it forth. Now is the time to be in Union.

Know yourself as the graceful Being that you are. Let your grace carry you effortlessly everywhere.

MY FIRE

I am telling you, I was *fire!*

I love to talk about my fire, my passion. It was deep and intense in me.

Yes, I was gentleness, grace and compassion, but every single facet of me was born from the heat of my fire. It was my absolute passion to do what I was doing. I had given my whole life to studying and preparing myself for my ministry. I did not retreat to a cave or a mountain top so that I could blend myself with God in that fashion. Instead I chose to go forth into humanity, to speak, to demonstrate my purpose, to take God to the people, and to bring the people to God.

I stirred the waters! Believe me, I stirred the waters relentlessly. I was not a passive man. I opened my heart and I opened my mouth, too. I was filled to overflowing with fire and I expressed myself boldly. There was nothing quiet or tepid about me. In my telling of the Truth for all of you to hear, many did not like it. My words were not words of judgment, but those who needed to protect their illusions felt threatened by me. I was a revolutionary. That was a fact!

Recognize, for a moment, the mark I left in history. Recognize how deep a mark it was—and still is. Could I have left such a mark or had such influence if I had been a quiet, passive man? No! It was my fire that enabled me to carve my way through the dense layers of consciousness at that time and seed the light so clearly and substantially. It was the fire of my passion that carried those seeds and drove them into the Earth and into your energies. It was my fire that made love so potent in my life.

My lifetime was a divine experience for me. It was transforming on all levels. I have spoken often of my joy, and it still resounds clearly through my heart. Understand with me, that I left no part of my expression untouched. I loved and cared so very deeply and gave myself free rein to express this. I did not hide my caring, I did not hide my light. I did the opposite. I trusted it and rode it thoroughly. And in turn, it gave me, and all of you, intense pleasure.

It was my joy to be so bold and so forthright. It was my joy to speak so brazenly about the goodness in all people and the love that ties us all together. It was my love to love in all the ways that I possibly could. I gave myself complete freedom, and because of this, I was inspired, vital and fulfilled.

When you think of me, don't just remember my gentleness and compassion. Also remember me as a man of passion and vision and blazing bright spirit! Remember me as being full of the life and intensity of fire! Remember the spark in my eyes and the deep love reverberating in my voice. Think of me as a man who loved, who laughed, who listened, who cried, who comforted, who cared and who was, yes, very, very funny! I was all man, just like I was all God. Heaven and Earth were one and the same in my heart and body.

Remember, I was *real!* I was honest, simple and dedicated. I was a man—a man with a mission! Know that I fulfilled this mission with all the fire in my soul. It was glorious and I did it thoroughly and exceedingly well. I knew I was on Earth to "torch the way of light through the darkness," and this I did. It was my fire that has enabled this light to grow into the present.

God is my passion. God is my fire. My devotion to God is endless and my eagerness to express this is always immediate in me. It is my life. How could it be otherwise? It is who I am.

You are fire also! You have been afraid of this because you know it is powerful and intense. Don't be afraid now. Give up fear because there is nothing in you of which to be afraid. Your fire is your life force, your enthusiasm and your deep love revealed. It is you telling your Truth with confidence and conviction.

You care about life as much as I do. You want to give life, touch life, admire life, nurture life. You want to wake up the light in everyone as much as I do. How can you help it? It is your passion as well.

Be your fire! Live the passion of your depths and feel the ecstasy and peace that comes to you as a result of expressing your Truth and creating from this powerful substance. Spread it around amongst yourselves, your families, your world. Love openly and with exuberance.

Now is YOUR time!

NOW, YOU CAN BLAZE YOUR GLORY. Hallelujah!

YOU ARE THE MESSIAH

YOU, THE PEOPLE, *ARE* THE MESSIAH! You always have been but you just didn't realize it.

If any of you are waiting for me to come back, I am not coming. How would that serve? You have already known me well in the physical. I have served, and continue to serve, as a loving role model for you.

I have already planted my teachings into the ethers of the planet. There is no need for me to come forth to repeat myself. This does not mean that I do not manifest my energies on Earth in very material ways from time to time, to remind all of you that you yourselves are the light. But, waiting for me to show up as the next "guiding light"—this will never happen.

You, yourselves, are already the "guiding lights." You carry within you all the glories of God of which I ever spoke and embodied. You now know this in yourselves. It is for you to awaken your own body of light through the form of your own material essence. For me to return would be an insult to your brilliance. It would be like a parent who could never stop parenting. You have no need of me. You only have need of yourselves.

All conditions are right now for you to fully know and spring forth from your brilliance, your essence, your overflowing well of light. The veils of illusion that have separated you from your sacred Truth are lifting. They are lifting right now as we speak together. This is because *it is time!* The energies of your civilization call this to themselves and you are awakening as bright stars exploding into the universe for all to see. You are not asleep any more. You are not passive. You are not numb.

When people speak of the "next Messiah" coming, what are they really saying? Are they saying that they are waiting for someone to come who will, by his very presence, give the signal for everyone to be lit up, to be joyous, to be creative, to be knowing of the God within themselves? Are they living in some kind of internal "waiting room?" Is this room filled only with struggle and pain? Is the day the next Messiah comes the day that people will take themselves down from their crosses? Is that the day they will take me down from my own? What have *you* been thinking was going to happen when the next Messiah showed up? Peace in the world? Peace in your own heart? Fulfillment?

Only those who do not feel powerful need a Messiah; only those who do not feel that they have grace and dominion over their lives are waiting for someone or something from the outside to come and save them. They believe they need someone, someone who knows more and who is closer to God; someone who is the face and figurehead of God incarnate; someone who is the giver of grace and salvation. These people are living lives of fear and desperation. They feel they need a "special agent" to be the middle person between them and God. They believe they need a messenger.

What I am saying to you now is that you don't need a messenger. You don't need a special agent. You don't need someone who already embodies the qualities that you associate with a higher, more spiritualized, Godly person. *You only need yourselves, because you already are all of these things!*

What are you waiting for? You already have it in you now. You already *are* the very substance that makes any and all of this possible. It has already been planted inside of you. You were this the very day you were created by that which seeded life in you. What is there to wait for outside of yourself now? Nothing. Because no one is coming.

The gift you bring to this plane of Earth is exactly like the gift I brought to Earth so long ago. Would you have wanted or expected me to withhold all of that light blazing through me? Of course not! Neither can you ask for nor expect that of yourselves. You *need* to shine.

Gather your internal resources together now. Reach inside for all that you have sensed within you that you have not yet claimed or shared. Touch your Self inside. Touch those places and spaces where you *truly* live. Let go of the persona and the material wrapping around you; it has served to shield and protect you and enabled you to stay hidden for as long as you deemed necessary. Seize that within you which is *real*.

You are awake to your light. This power carries itself right through your bodies and streams out your fingers and your toes, your eyes and mouths, your hearts and your minds. You are one with the Christ. You *are* the Christ. You *are* the Messiah!

Go on, have it for yourself! Take it! Be it! Own it!

NOW IS YOUR TIME

I challenge you now. LIVE THE MESSIAH THAT YOU ARE!
Go beyond acceptance into full, deliberate, enthusiastic living of
this magnificent truth.

Radiate your fire. Radiate your beauty. Radiate your clarity and
transform your lives into absolute joy and well-Being. Radiate your
ecstasy every morning because today is yet another gift to "make
hay while the sun is shining." Rise up and walk out into the world
boldly and in your full grace. Speak up and take positive, loving,
direct action. Use your God-given power to create the beauty, love,
harmony, health, wealth, happiness and unity that you have always
talked about. Radiate your divine power to create patterns of brilliance that unite all of life. Empower yourselves and better your
world now. *Live your Mastery!*

Love yourself and your world into union. Unite heaven and
Earth as one.

Do you think this is beyond your scope of capability? Not anymore. Living in your full power enables you to do all of this with
joy, vitality and success. Sometimes you will do it through overt
action; other times it will be purely the energetic radiance of your
love spreading itself across the globe.

Please accept my challenge, not for my sake but for yours. It is
an invitation of love, to love. It is the most profound gift you will
ever give yourself.

MY FINAL MESSAGE

Great Beings, I salute you.

We have come to the end of our journey in this form. You have been given much material to think about, digest and build upon in the days to come. Give yourselves plenty of time and space to let this all settle where it needs and wants to settle.

I have so enjoyed being with you in this process. It has been a precious gift for me to feel you opening inside and setting yourself free. You have been courageous and persevering. It is beautiful to feel the old ways and structures built in my name loosening their hold. We have both grown much in two thousand years. It is time for all of that to change.

We have great honor and respect for each other, you and I. We have whole lives ahead of us, many roads yet to explore, vast creativity yet to express. We are each unfolding. Knowing that we are always joined in our hearts means we are together no matter where we find ourselves. We continue to learn, to laugh, to teach and to inspire one another as we breath our mighty radiance and send it spinning joyously into the ethers of creation. Wherever it lands, new light is born.

You know how much I love this Earth. You know how much I love mankind. You know how happy it makes me to co-create with so many strong, eager, sacred, loving Beings such as yourselves.

You are on Earth with as much purpose as I was two thousand years ago. Conditions are different now, times are different now. As I have told you, everything is right and ripe now for you to express yourselves freely and safely.

You are the New World. Each of you is the Messiah manifest, and glory is blazing on Earth now because of it. Be prepared for some big changes. Be prepared to make these changes!

You are great leaders with great vision; you are gracing Earth with your passion and power. Your love is potent, direct, healing, uplifting and illuminating. You are resourceful and magnetic. You are skillfully manifesting your visions and sending forth your insight to ensure that your plans have the future in mind. All the bridges you build today will be used with gratitude tomorrow. You are a great force of light that gifts all of life. Your children and their children will bless you.

Brothers and sisters, we are one family united in love and freedom. Our task is to be ourselves and to blaze our joy far and wide. We can all do it exceedingly well, with passion, pleasure, peace and purpose.

Know that you are loved by me, by all of life everywhere. Open yourselves now to the inpouring of love from all of us. Open yourselves to our gracious love as we fill your hearts with our joy and our gratitude for you. Touch and be touched. Inspire and be inspired. Heal and be healed. Love and be loved. Celebrate and be celebrated! We are free! Hallelujah!

In the name of God, now let us join hands.

Dear God, these are great and mighty Beings whose hands I now hold. They are brilliant in their light and their hearts are strong and giving and honest. These are simple people wanting to live simple lives of joy and devotion that are ignited by Truth.

Dear God, keep these mighty Beings safe always. Show them how beautiful they are. Open their eyes to their vast power and joyousness. Open their ears to their deep wisdom and understanding. Open their hearts to their courage and confidence, to their endless love, their sweet compassion. Open their feet to walk proudly upon the earth with strength, dignity and grace.

Dear God, let them know how cherished they are at every moment of every day. And love them fully, for they are your children.

Dear God, we know that you do this so very well. Amen.

PEACE

Our Closing Message

In closing, we dedicate this book to you, dear reader, for your grace and courage in taking this journey with us. We thank you for being one of many who are consciously and deliberately opening your hearts to exemplify that all human beings are the glory and transcendence of the Christ crystal in physical form. Each one of us is this perfection radiating visibly right here and now.

Your reading of this book has altered you and altered the patterns of the world. You might be asking yourself, "How could this be? It's just a book." However, this body of energy called "a book" is a vehicle carrying the intent of rebirth. Its purpose is vast and far reaching. It is fueled and supported by the strength and dedication to God of many dimensions. As you have cleansed yourselves and shifted your own archaic patterns, the restoration of light is happening instantly. This change is impacting all humans, all life forms and the globe as a whole. It is happening right now. This is a tribute to the power of your God-love.

In reading about and igniting your own deep joy of liberation and the creations which can now spring forth from this, you have added your love and your grace to the energy of a world of peace, self-respect and freedom. You have added your vital energy to the new matrix of higher truth and divinity through which all humans will be able to see and understand themselves. You have helped anchor positive patterns for everyone. With your strength and your devotion, you have helped build a bridge for the inspiration of God to physically manifest. This is co-creation at its highest. For this, we are deeply grateful.

We know that your light will become more potent as you continue to deepen and expand. In parting, we encourage you to let go and allow everything that has transpired here to settle gently where it will. There is plenty of time to get to know yourself. You will be guided by your wisdom and valiant light every step of the way.

GODSPEED

EPILOGUE

Having fulfilled the intention of this book which was to focus solely on Jesus, we want to say a few words about Mary and Master Saint Germain and their part in this project.

Subsequent to the first year of teaching the Ascended Master I intensive, Mary came to the forefront and we developed Ascended Master II. Although this beloved teacher has been widely explored and experienced by many of us, the quality of her energy and the purpose of her work in this intensive was unexpected and unique. She presented herself in a way that was unlike anything we had heard, felt or seen before. Exploring her in reference to her role specifically in Jesus' life was extraordinary. We feel this piece is another vital link to the repatterning of new consciousness.

In our third year, Master Saint Germain brought forth his intensive, and this took us to yet another level of clarity and refinement. We could see the perfection of these three Beings—Jesus, Mary and Saint Germain—and the design of what they were doing. It became very obvious that people needed to clear both the Jesus and the Mary energy before being able to receive the dynamic, action-oriented impulse of Saint Germain. Without the way cleared, he would not be fully received.

Our experience of Master Saint Germain is that he is here to get things done! He reflects the wizard, the wise man, the magician, the creator, the shape-shifter in all of us. He has lived many lives on Earth and knows the terrain exceedingly well. Through his teaching and explosive inspiration, we can connect with, and successfully exercise, our own dynamic creativity. He is the perfect agent to be the bridge between the old and the new.

In New Age circles, people are drawn to Saint Germain like a magnet. Many times, we have had participants attend our Jesus and Mary intensives just so they could get to Saint Germain! His requirement with us is that participants have to clear their way through Jesus and Mary first.

We have not yet mentioned Sananda. For those of you who are unfamiliar with this name, Sananda is the present-day energy that was Jesus. Just as all of us will be more expanded two thousand years from now, so Jesus has grown to become a larger presence—Sananda. Jesus is but one of his incarnations.

Toward the end of the Lightstar Program, Jesus came to Deborah one day and asked her if she would do an "updated" portrait of him. She relates, "I was up on Mount Shasta in the cabin one day, and Jesus came to me. I found myself admiring his robe and his traditional garb to which I usually didn't pay much attention. As I was thinking how beautiful he looked, he asked me, 'Would you be willing to do a portrait of me as I look now?'

"No sooner had I thought to reply, 'Yes' when he turned around, whipped off his long hair and his robe and stood there in a golden, glowing body suit with a bald head and a huge golden disc pulsating in his third eye! I was speechless! This was Jesus, MY Jesus!? After a second or two came the thought, 'Well, probably I will look radically different in two thousand years! So, okay, I'll adjust!'

"The portrait was born right before the four Lightstar interns left Lighthouse and we all recognized the significance of this. It marked the transition from the past to the present."

We have no position about people embracing Sananda versus Jesus. They radiate different levels of the same exquisite energy and we continue to experience both of them depending upon our focus and purpose. Jesus' energy is more Earth and ground; Sananda's is more universality and cosmos. Ultimately, they are simply reflecting what we need in the moment. One is not better than the other. Each serves its purpose.

In our Ascended Master I intensive, we include the energy of Sananda. We have found that some participants want to skip right to the Sananda energy without facing and embracing Jesus. This will never work. We each must first go into, and through, the Jesus experience in order to fully appreciate and absorb the Sananda vibration. It is similar to pretending that Mary does not include Jesus. Every piece is a vital part of ourselves played out by and reflected through each of them.

We deliberately did not make mention of Sananda earlier in this book because we did not want to distract you, the reader, from the critical task at hand—clearing and healing your energy about Jesus. In the future, we plan to write other books devoted to the energies of Mary, Master Saint Germain and Sananda.

About the Authors

Since 1985, Deborah and Jack Bartello have been conducting workshops in spiritual development throughout the United States. They are both creative leaders and seers in their own right and joyously offer their assistance in facilitating others in their spiritual awakening. The strength of their union as a couple goes far beyond the traditional definition of relationship. What makes their coupling unique is their complete and utter devotion to spirit. They realize their relationship is not about self, but about God, their higher purpose and the "higher good." They believe we are all here to shine and are committed toward this end both in themselves and everyone they meet.

In addition to their workshops together, Deborah is a visionary artist and has developed programs on interdimensional creativity. For more information on their programs, tapes and visionary artwork write:

Project Enlightenment

P.O. Box 1497, Mount Shasta, CA 96067.

Also, please visit the Project Enlightenment website at:

www.projectenlightenment.com,

or email them at: jd@projectenlightenment.com.